transform
your **life**

Property of
HarperCollins*Publishers*
on loan to

Hilton

If you wish find out more about our
books, please do so via our website,
www.**fire**and**water**.com

transform
your **life**

10 steps to real results

Carole Gaskell

Thorsons

Thorsons
An Imprint of HarperCollins*Publishers*
77–85 Fulham Palace Road
Hammersmith, London W6 8JB

The Thorsons website address is: www.thorsons.com

Published by Thorsons 2000

1 3 5 7 9 10 8 6 4 2

© Carole Gaskell 2000

Carole Gaskell asserts the moral right to
be identified as the author of this work

A catalogue record for this book
is available from the British Library

ISBN 0 00 710078 7

Printed and bound in Great Britain by
Martins the Printers Ltd, Berwick upon Tweed

☆ To my Dad who taught me that anything is possible if you set your mind to it; to my Mum who taught me to open my heart and trust my intuition; and to my sisters, Helen, Fiona and Jilly, who have helped me to understand the power of synergy, wherever we are in our lives and in the world.

☆ Also to my friends, clients and colleagues who enrich my life and remind me there's something new we can learn every day. Here's to enjoying the journey of life step by step, moment by moment – now.

☆ *The will to win, the desire to succeed, the urge to reach your full potential, these are the keys to unlock the door to personal excellence.* ☆

Eddie Robinson

Contents

Acknowledgements: 8

Introduction: 9
    Your New Life Starts *Now*! 10

The 10-Step Process

Part 1: Preparing your Launch Pad 25

    Step 1: See the Bigger Picture 27
    Step 2: Build the Right Foundations 49
    Step 3: Spring Clean your Life 71
    Step 4: Value your True Essence 87
    Step 5: Focus on What Really Matters 105

Part 2: Real Results 121

    Step 6: Clarify your Vision and Goals 123
    Step 7: Make Time Work for You 143
    Step 8: Shape Up your Finances 165
    Step 9: Attract the Relationships You Want 187
    Step 10: Get into the Flow 213

Further Reading 229

Further Information 233
About the Author 234

Acknowledgements

This book has been inspired by the wisdom of many people from both my personal and professional life. I would particularly like to thank Rob Murray, Thomas Leonard, Laura Berman-Fortgang, Sandy Vilas, Chris Barrow, Paul Henry, my coaching colleagues and clients and CoachU for their inspiration.

introduction

☆ *It only takes one person to change your life – you.* ☆

Ruth Casey

Your New Life Starts *Now*!

Are you itching to do something new? Do you have a dream you'd like to fulfil? Are you setting up or growing a business or looking for career success? Do you want more balance in your life? Do you need to create more space to think about life decisions? Do you feel restless or does something not feel quite right – but you're not sure what? Are you looking for a greater sense of purpose?

Each one of us can transform our life in a split second by doing something differently, taking action or thinking in a new way. Buying this book means you've made the perfect start, so let's get going – your new life starts *now*!

Your Own Lifecoach

I am a lifecoach – that means I act as a catalyst, partnering people as they transform their lives. I help people to bring out their personal best, to clarify where they are now, where they want to be and how to get there. As you read this book I will be *your* lifecoach and guide you through a tried and tested 10-step process to help you achieve real results. Whether you're looking for more time, more balance, less stress, greater self-confidence, better relationships, financial security, career and business success or a more fulfilling life, I'll encourage you to transform your life – on your terms.

You're the expert on your life and like an effective coach I'll be asking you great questions, challenging you and helping you to uncover your own wisdom. In this book you can explore your own thoughts, see yourself as you really are and draw up plans, monitor your progress and create the life you really want.

There are times when life can be a stimulating and invigorating experience and others when it can feel stagnant, even difficult. Sometimes it's easy to settle for an okay job, a mediocre relationship or a semi-convenient lifestyle. We're all so busy, it's often easier to accept second best, to run few risks and achieve few real successes. As Henry Thoreau said, 'The mass of men lead lives of quiet desperation.' This is *not* what I want for you. I want you to feel inspired by your life and excited about your future.

As we work together, I'll encourage you to open your mind to see yourself and your life in a new way. The more you transform yourself on the inside, the more benefits you'll see on the outside. As you become more aware of how you learn and behave, you'll find it easier to coach yourself! Lifecoaching is an action-orientated process and although it can often enhance your self-understanding, it's not a substitute for counselling. Coaches don't tend to work on 'issues' or focus on the past but rather on where you are now and the future you want to create for yourself. To a certain degree lifecoaching is very much based on common sense. Its tools and techniques do work – I see evidence of it almost every day.

Take a look at the following quiz and see how coaching can help you to transform your life.

☆ *You don't get to choose how you're going to die, or when. You can only decide how you're going to live. Now.* ☆

Joan Baez

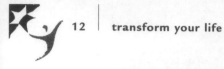

Quick Transformation Quiz

Answer the questions below by ticking the appropriate box and calculating your score as follows:
2 points = Yes/Agree/Not Applicable, 1 point = Agree sometimes, 0 point = No/Disagree

		YES	SOMETIMES	NO
1	My work and personal life are in balance.			☑
2	I have plenty of time to do the things I want.			☑
3	I have regular habits that support and nurture me.			☑
4	I have relatively little stress in my life.			☑
5	I am relaxed about money and/or I am earning what I deserve.			☑
6	I have a team of friends/family/colleagues who support me.			☑
7	I have simplified my life and things run smoothly.			☑
8	I love my work and have a career strategy that is working.			☑
9	I am an ideal weight and shape for me.	☑		
10	I have plenty of self-confidence and a positive attitude towards life.			☑
11	I am happy and fulfilled in my personal and professional life.			☑
12	I sleep well, eat a well-balanced diet and I exercise as much as I need.		☑	
13	I am not afraid of saying 'no'.		☑	
14	I am excited about the future and have a life-plan that inspires me.		☑	
15	I am clear about my personal and professional goals.			☑
16	I know what my needs and values are.		☑	☑
17	I make the most of every opportunity I have – I miss nothing.			☑
18	My home/work environment is well-organized and inspiring.			☑
19	I never do something because I feel I should or ought to.		☑	
20	I know clearly where I want to be in one year's time.			☑

7p

If you scored 0–20 points

You're confident with some areas of your life, but could drastically improve in others. You stand to achieve the maximum benefit from lifecoaching in both your personal and your professional life. This book will help you to make the changes you want to transform your life, strengthen your support framework, establish your strengths and values, clarify your personal vision and tap into your true potential.

If you scored 21–30 points

Well done! Life is presumably pretty good for you. However, you probably suffer from the occasional stumbling block and suspect that you could achieve much more, both personally and professionally. This book will support you in clearing your way towards being more effective and achieving a balanced integration of your home and work life. Don't wait too long – you're almost there!

If you scored 31–40 points

Congratulations! You're obviously close to reaching your full potential. You probably know what your vision and goals are and have a plan for achieving them. This book may inspire you to achieve the last 10 or 20 per cent. This could be just the kick-start you need to go the final distance.

Initial Score ☐ **Score on Completion of Step 1** ☐

Final Score on Completion of Book ☐

My Own Experience

People often ask me how I got involved in coaching and what qualifies me to be a coach. The answer is simple – lifecoaching is something I 'evolved' into over many years. I've been interested in people and what makes them tick for as long as I can remember. I enjoyed a successful career in marketing, learning to understand people's needs and identifying new business opportunities. Business and personal development became a passion for me. In my spare time I attended many courses, devoured development books and studied counselling and various complementary therapies. I was extremely fortunate to work in the entertainment industry, where I met many successful people who had followed their hearts and had created very successful lives for themselves. They inspired me and I learned much from them.

However, as my career developed, my personal life started to suffer. I never had enough time to do the things I wanted to. I worked in London for many years and spent over three hours a day commuting. I was involved in floating a company on the stock exchange and I worked long hours and sacrificed my health and relationships in the process. Increasingly I started to think, 'There has to be more to life than this.'

It was whilst working for a short period in the US that I first came across life-coaching. An extremely successful advertising executive in New York told me how he'd been disillusioned, overworked, stressed out and 'empty' until his life had been transformed by working with a coach. It wasn't until that moment that I realized how much I'd lost sight of the important things in my own life.

Back in the UK, I began to work with a coach of my own and our sessions helped me to bring my life back into balance. I started to make my own well-being my number one priority and reconnect with what mattered most to me. It took a lot of work to gain a clear understanding of who I am and what I want in life – and I'm still learning. But my life was touched so deeply by coaching that I eventually decided to become a lifecoach myself. I studied with the world's leading coach-training organization, CoachU, and was extremely lucky to be mentored by some of the best lifecoaches. Now I don't live a perfect life, but I am aware of what that would be for me and am moving closer and closer towards it. I'm aware every day that the life I live is my own choice. The more choices I make, the freer I become and ultimately the more fulfilled I am. That's what I want for myself – and that's what I want for you, too.

Transforming your life can take as long as you want. If you have specific objectives you'd like to achieve quickly, let's rise to the challenge! Equally, if you see transformation as a lifelong process, there's no reason why you can't enjoy the steps along the path. It's your life, so design it the way you want it to be! Acknowledge your dreams, take some simple steps to start yourself off and then keep going! As the saying goes, even a journey of 1,000 miles begins with one step.
Here's to transforming your life!
Enjoy it!

Carole Gaskell

The 10-Step Process

For easy reference the 10-step process is in two parts:

☆ **Part 1: Preparing your Launch Pad**, Steps 1–5, focuses on helping you to build firm foundations from which you can lift off and transform your life. You'll be looking at who you are, who you want to be and what's important to you.

☆ **Part 2: Real Results**, Steps 6–10, will take you through an effective action plan, enabling you to achieve the real results you want in your life.

Part 1: Preparing your Launch Pad

☆ **Step 1: See the Bigger Picture** will set you up for success by helping you to see your life from a new perspective, encouraging you to develop invaluable qualities to take your life to the next level and reminding you of the importance of picturing the results you want at the beginning.

☆ **Step 2: Build the Right Foundations** will ensure you establish a strong power base from which to launch the next phase of your life. You'll be inspired to take good care of yourself, create an inspiring environment and develop a powerful framework of support around you.

☆ **Step 3: Spring Clean your Life** will empower you to de-sludge and de-clutter, streamlining your life so that you gain more energy, space and clarity. You'll be encouraged to remove any distractions and obstacles likely to block your way ahead.

☆ **Step 4: Value your True Essence** will get you to focus on your achievements and strengths, delegate your weaknesses and connect with your own special essence.

☆ **Step 5: Focus on What Really Matters** is the final element of your launch pad. Here you'll learn how to identify your values, be encouraged to set well-defined boundaries and high personal standards and clarify what is truly important to you.

Part 2: Real Results

☆ **Step 6: Clarify your Vision and Goals** will encourage you to 'think big' as you create your vision, connect with your dreams, clarify your intentions and define your goals.

☆ **Step 7: Make Time Work for You** will see you starting to plan ahead. You'll learn how to manage yourself superbly so you achieve more in less time.

☆ **Step 8: Shape Up your Finances** gets you to look at your money situation, strengthen your financial foundations and establish ways of propelling yourself forward financially.

☆ **Step 9: Attract the Relationships You Want** will help you to determine what relationships you want, understand your needs and how to get them met, improve your powers of communication and become more attractive to yourself and others so that you can harness the power of synergy in your life.

☆ **Step 10: Get into the Flow** inspires you to pull the whole process together and gives you the confidence to live in the land of

opportunity. Connecting your *powerful* foundations with your *big* vision and your *small* steps will enable you to take action to bring your plans into reality, create momentum and get into the flow of transforming your life!

There is a huge difference between understanding the theory and putting it into practice. The real value in coaching is the role it plays in empowering you to take *action* to do what you say you want to do. But once you've taken the first few steps you'll find that you (and your life) will start to gather momentum. It may take time to fully integrate all the elements of transformation, but the more steps you take, the more you'll find yourself 'in the flow' and the sooner you'll start enjoying the life you really want.

The Format of Each Step

For ease of reference, each step follows the same pattern. Every chapter begins with a brief **Overview** of the step and a clear indication of the results you're likely to achieve when you've completed it. If you can picture the end result at the beginning, you'll have a greater chance of bringing it into reality!

Next comes the **Personal Reward** section where I ask you to write down how you'll reward yourself when you've finished the step. The completion of each step is a significant milestone along your path of transformation and I want you to recognize it as such. Acknowledging your progress to date is a valuable lesson in itself! As you go through a process of change it's very easy to drive yourself forward, focus on what's next and overlook what you've already achieved. It's important to give yourself rewards as you go. Treats could include a night out with friends, a massage, a box of chocolates, a long walk, a trip to a health club – you decide. Celebrate the little wins as well as the big ones and enjoy your transformation process.

This is followed by a **Quick Transformation Quiz** of 20 questions. Note your score as you begin each step and again when you've completed it. The maximum score on each quiz is 40 points. My challenge is for you to score a minimum of 32 points on every quiz once you've completed the book!

Each step then features **Five Sections**, each represented by a star. These include a combination of information, quotes, questions and assignments. As you complete each section, colour in your step by step progress tracker (*see page 22*).

Then there are **Key Insights Gained from the Step**, where you can list the five most valuable insights you've learned from each step. Doing this will help you to commit these core elements to memory. Just write down key words or even draw a picture to remind yourself of the important points.

As well as insights, in **Quick Wins Gained from the Step** you can list breakthroughs and changes you've already started to make to enhance your life, and in **The Action Steps You Now Agree to Take** you can list the actions you're now willing to take to transform your life.

Finally, for each step there are **Real Results** – some life histories to inspire you!

☆ *Take the first step in faith.*

You don't have to see the whole

staircase, just take the first step. ☆

Martin Luther King

Getting the Most out of the 10 Steps

Just by reading, absorbing the information and following the exercises, you'll begin to actually experience the benefits of lifecoaching. You are the creator of your life, no one else, so the more effort you put into answering the quizzes and questions and taking action on the assignments, the more results you're likely to achieve. Why not start now? It's never too early (or too late) to start to transform your life!

Familiarize Yourself with the Process

Before you start going through the steps in detail, you might find it useful to quickly skim over the chapters to familiarize yourself with the process. The steps themselves can be followed in sequence or you may prefer to focus on the sections that appeal to you the most. Go with whatever works best for you. Some people find that following two steps in parallel can work very well. (You may be tempted to skip over the steps in Part 1, but I would strongly advise against this, as you'll find the insights you gain from Steps 1 to 5 will strengthen you and save you time in the long run.)

Like anything in life, some concepts in the book will work brilliantly for you while others may have little value. We all respond to things in different ways. If you find yourself stuck on a step, making no headway, leave it. Take what works for you and leave the rest. But stay open-minded and give yourself the opportunity to see things afresh. You could be pleasantly surprised by the results!

As life is constantly changing and moving in cycles, you may find you want to revisit a step several times. The process can provide the structure for a regular review that you can return to year after year as you perfect different elements of your life.

Progress at your own Pace

Remember, there's no rush. Whether the changes you are making are fast or slow, subtle or fundamental, it's up to you. But even small changes can have a significant impact over the long term!

Make Yourself Accountable to Someone

No man is an island and one of the great benefits of lifecoaching is the synergy between the coach and client. People can often achieve a lot more by pooling their resources and supporting each other – two heads can be better than one. Bearing this in mind, I suggest you get the support of someone – perhaps a friend, family member, work colleague or even a coach – as you work through this book. You'll derive great benefits from sharing your thoughts and insights with another person.

Any process of change will, at some point, bring you face to face with thoughts or issues that you would perhaps prefer not to look at and your support person may also be able to help you with these 'growing pains'.

Your helper will act as a constant reminder of who you want to be and what you want to achieve. You need someone who will stand by you through thick and thin, someone you can trust to support you, hold you to your commitments, and keep you on track.

☆ I want to make myself accountable to:

Allow Yourself 'Quiet Time' to Think Things Through

When working through the 10 steps, after reading a specific section you might want to stop and ponder for a while. I actively encourage you to do this. Sometimes it's during the gaps between our thoughts that we gain the real answers to our life's questions.

To do this, I suggest that you take yourself to a quiet inspirational place in your home. You might want to play your favourite music, sit in your favourite chair, light a candle, look at your favourite view – do whatever is necessary for you to fully access your thoughts. If you prefer, a visit to your local café or park or a drive in your car might spark your imagination and give you the answers you're looking for. Remember, the answers are inside you, so the more comfortable and 'at one' you feel with your environment, the easier you'll find it to open yourself up, increase your awareness and draw the answers to you.

Keep your insights in a Journal or Notebook

As you work through this programme you'll probably want to make notes or jot down your answers to some of the questions. You'll find it useful to keep all your thoughts, insights and action plans together in a journal or notebook – so why not treat yourself to one now, before you begin?

Here's to the first day of the rest of your life!

☆ *Twenty years from now you will be more disappointed by the things that you didn't do than by the ones you did do. So throw off the bowlines. Sail away from the safe harbour. Catch the trade winds in your sails. Explore. Dream. Discover.* ☆

Mark Twain

Step by Step Progress Tracker

As you work through the steps track your progress by colouring in each star section as you complete it.

Part One: Preparing your Launch Pad

	Commitment	Perspective	Current Reality	Characteristics to Develop	Expected Results
Step 1	☆	☆	☆	☆	☆

	Self-Care	Regular Habits	Support Team	Inspirational Environment	Resources
Step 2	☆	☆	☆	☆	☆

	De-Sludge	Obstacles	Limiting Beliefs	Past Lessons	Take Charge
Step 3	☆	☆	☆	☆	☆

	Accomplishments	Strengths	Purpose	Unique Value	True Essence
Step 4	☆	☆	☆	☆	☆

	Ideal Life	Identify Values	Express Values	Boundaries	Standards
Step 5	☆	☆	☆	☆	☆

Part Two: Real Results

	Vision	Goals	Intentions	Steps	Action Plans
Step 6	☆	☆	☆	☆	☆

	Reality Check	Planning	Priorities	Time Wasters	Manage Yourself
Step 7	☆	☆	☆	☆	☆

	Financial Reality	Reserves	Blocks	Money Goals	Prosperity
Step 8	☆	☆	☆	☆	☆

	Current Relationships	Ideal Relationships	Understand Needs	Tackle Blocks	Attraction
Step 9	☆	☆	☆	☆	☆

	Progress Review	Flow	Synchronicity	Let Go	Momentum
Step 10	☆	☆	☆	☆	☆

preparing

your
launch pad

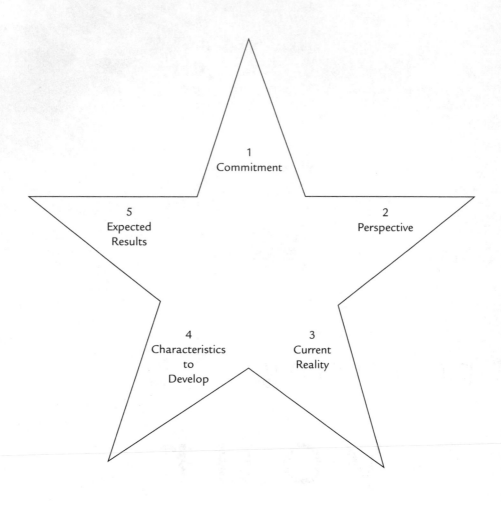

see the
bigger
picture

☆ *Change your thoughts and you change your world.* ☆

Norman Vincent Peale

Overview

The perfect place to start your life transformation is with you. Who you are on the inside has a clear correlation with what your life is like on the outside. The more you understand yourself and the more you're aware of the key dynamics in your life, the easier you'll find it to implement the insights you gain from the lifecoaching process.

In Step 1 you'll start by confirming your commitment to transforming your life and putting things into context by looking at your life from a broader perspective. You'll establish where you are now and be encouraged to look at your own attitudes and behaviour and the characteristics you need to develop to get the most out of your transformation process. You will become more aware of how your own thoughts and actions shape your life. The more willing you are to develop a positive way of thinking, the smoother you'll find the ride of your life becomes.

The final element in this step is to picture the results you want to achieve. Once you're clear about what you want, you can determine the most effective way of making it happen.

When you've completed this step:

☆ You'll have confirmed your commitment to transform your life.

☆ You'll have stepped back from your immediate life and addressed some 'bigger picture' issues which we'll revisit later in the book.

☆ You'll have established what your life looks like now.

☆ You'll be clearer about the qualities you need to develop to make your transformation easier.

☆ You'll have started to clarify the results you want to achieve in the next phase of your life.

Personal Reward for Completing Step 1

☆ Write down here how you will reward yourself when you have completed Step 1:

Quick Transformation Quiz

Answer the questions below by ticking the appropriate box and calculating your score as follows:

2 points = Yes/Agree/Not Applicable, 1 point = Agree sometimes, 0 point = No/Disagree

		YES	SOMETIMES	NO
1	I take full responsibility for what happens to me in life.	☑	☐	☐
2	I know I always have a choice.	☐	☑	☑
3	I have a positive attitude to life.	☐	☐	☑
4	Where appropriate I am willing to take risks.	☑	☐	☐
5	I am honest and truthful with myself.	☐	☑	☐
6	I do not lie nor am I deceptive in my dealings with others.	☑	☐	☐
7	I never do something because I feel I should or ought to.	☐	☑	☐
8	I believe that my life can change as I change my attitudes and my beliefs.	☑	☐	☐
9	I am courageous and have plenty of inner strength.	☐	☑	☐
10	I have a clear sense of who I am and what I believe in.	☐	☐	☑
11	I hold myself accountable and keep my word 99 per cent of the time.	☐	☑	☐
12	I am able to sit back when necessary and see the bigger picture of my life.	☐	☐	☑
13	I realize I'm only human and accept my weaknesses as well as my strengths.	☐	☐	☑

		YES	SOMETIMES	NO
14	I open myself up to new opportunities and am ready for the unexpected.	☐	☑	☐
15	I am willing and able to trust my own intuition.	☐	☑	☐
16	I don't undermine my own worth by comparing myself with others.	☐	☐	☑
17	I am willing to learn from the lessons in my past.	☑	☐	☐
18	I am fully committed to doing what it takes to live the life I want.	☑	☐	☐
19	The actions I take demonstrate my commitment and this is obvious to those around me.	☑	☐	☐
20	I can always be counted on to follow through and to meet previously agreed expectations.	☑	☐	☐

Initial Score ☐ 23 **Score on Completion of Step 1** ☐

Final Score on Completion of Book ☐

☆ *Dreams are renewable. No matter*

what our age or condition, there are

still untapped possibilities within us

and new beauty waiting to be born. ☆

Dale E. Turner

⭐ Confirm your Commitment

As you begin the 10-step process, it's important to acknowledge that whilst ideas, dreams and goals have a valuable place in your life, they're only as good as your commitment to achieving them. Are you ready to start taking the steps required to turn your ideas into reality? *Yes!!!*

☆ How committed are you to transforming your life?
  Rate yourself on a scale of 1 to 10, 1 being not particularly committed at all and 10 being totally committed:
  1 2 3 4 5 6 7 8 9 **10**

☆ How committed are you to actively participating in the exercises in this book? Again, 1 is not particularly committed and 10 totally committed:
  1 2 3 4 5 6 7 8 9 **10**

☆ How will you keep yourself disciplined to follow this process?

You may think that it will be hard to keep to your commitment, that you will not have enough time to do it. But when you take charge of your life, you *can* find sufficient time to work on yourself. Your day can include time to go for a jog or to the gym, to meditate, catch up with friends or family, develop a business plan, write a book or plan a holiday. . . It's a matter of making a choice and taking action! When you start a process like this, you'll find your life is not just changing during the time you read the book but during the 10,000 minutes of every week!

State your commitment to transformation by making a written agreement with yourself. Either use the following outline or develop your own wording to make your commitment more personal to you:

My Agreement to Transform my Life

I .Emma Josephine Lee........ am committed to transforming my life.
I understand I will get as much out of the process as I put into it and
that it's up to me to create my own value from each of the steps.
I acknowledge that a lot will be asked of me. I am willing to experiment with changing my behaviour, trying new things, reassessing
the assumptions and perceptions I hold, setting goals that are bigger,
removing sources of stress in my life and starting to redesign the way
I spend my time. I agree to complete the assignments to the best of
my ability and to take action on the plans I write.

I commit to devoting ...*several*... hours/days/weeks to transforming my life
I will be honest with myself when the going gets tough and will ask
for support when I realize I need it. Above all else I will relax, take
time, progress at my own pace and enjoy the process.

Your signature here ....

Date ....03/04/07...

Gain Perspective from the Bigger Picture

The first part of this step aims to get you thinking about yourself and your life
slightly differently. I'd like you to stand back for a moment and see the bigger
picture before you get down to some of the finer details of how you want to transform your life. I want you to allow yourself the space – and creativity – to see your
life from a broader perspective.

It's an incredibly useful experience every once in a while to lift yourself out of the day-
to-day pressures of your life and to look at things from a different vantage point. The

benefits might not be immediately apparent, but stick with it – as you progress through the book your answers to some of these early questions could well prove to be invaluable to you! Take some time now to answer the following questions:

Life Perspective Questions

If you were totally financially independent and money wasn't an issue for you, how would you spend your time? Be as specific as you can and write down what you would spend your time doing.

☆ Who are your top three heroes or role models (alive or dead)?
What do you admire most about them and why? *Gee – Patient, forgiving*
Dad – Calm, helping, trying
Frances – Caring, loving, understanding

☆ What are the three most important elements in your current life
and what did you do to make them possible?

☆ What experience in your life to date has become particularly
important to you? (This can be a positive or negative experience,
but either way, you know it has, or is likely to have, a significant
impact on your life.) *School, childhood, being teenager, eating disorders.*

☆ Fast-forward your life and imagine yourself as a fly on the wall at
your own funeral. How would you like to be remembered?
loving, caring, helpful, person who loved herself + others, laughing + smiling

☆ If you could choose a current problem or challenge in the
world today that you could be involved in seeking a solution for,
what would it be? *animal rights*

☆ If you could start your life again with a totally clean slate
but with the knowledge you've gained from all your experiences,
what would you do differently next time? *listened to myself,*
not look down on myself + felt embarrassed.

Establish Where You Are Now

Now consider your current life. The chances are it's hectic and complicated. Life is like that. Most of us are so busy, we rarely have time to think, let alone make long-term plans. Your days are probably jam-packed full of work, chores, dashing from A to B and back again. Perhaps you get up, dash madly around the house preparing for the day, drop the children off at school, commute to work, rush through your day-to-day tasks, pop out for shopping at lunchtime, maybe squeeze in a brief workout or hour with friends, and before you know it the day is over, only for you to repeat the whole process the next day. This probably isn't the way you want to live your life, is it? To help you find the time – and energy – to make changes, let's start by examining what your life currently looks like.

The Wheel of Life

The eight sections of the Wheel of Life represent a balanced wheel. Take the centre or hub of the wheel as 0 (totally dissatisfied) and the outer edge as 10 (totally satisfied). Rank your level of satisfaction with each area of your life by putting a cross on the relevant spoke. Draw a line to join the crosses together.

How balanced does the shape of your wheel look? Which of the areas of your life are you currently happy with? Where do you want to make improvements? (You might want to refer back to this wheel when you answer the questions at the end of this step.) Physical environment, friends/fam, money, career, fun

☆ *Everything changes when you change.* ☆

Jim Rohn

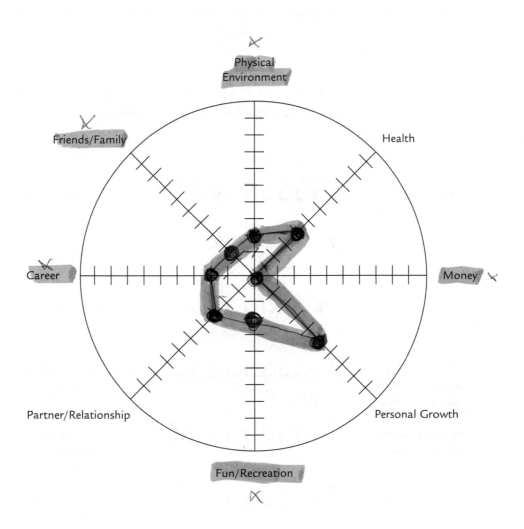

The Wheel of Life

Set Yourself Up for Success

As you begin to transform your life there are a variety of personal qualities I'd like you to develop to help make your transition into the next phase of your life as smooth as possible.

Take a look at the statements below and out of 10 rank yourself to indicate which of the two descriptions is nearest to the truth for you at the moment.

	1 2 3 4 5 6 7 8 9 10	
I blame others for what happens to me in life.	□□□□□□□☑□□ (8)	I take full responsibility for what happens to me in life.
I avoid facing the truth. There are gaps between what I say and what I do.	□□□□□□□☑□□ (8)	I have a fully developed sense of personal integrity and honesty and do exactly what I say.
I avoid making choices and tend to wait for things to happen to me.	□☑□□□□□□□□ (2)	I take the initiative and make my own choices.
I often think the cup is half empty and see the negative side of life.	☑□□□□□□□□□ (1)	I generally have a positive attitude. My cup is always half full.
I fear change and the unknown and never take risks.	□□□□□□□□□☑ (10)	I'm willing to extend my comfort zones, take calculated risks and step into the unknown.
I lack faith in myself and my ability to work things out.	☑□□□□□□□□□ (1)	I trust my own intuition and have faith in my own wisdom.
I have very little confidence.	☑□□□□□□□□□ (1)	I am confident and act as though I've already achieved what I want.

Select the qualities you want to work on.

Take Responsibility for your Life

We each hold our life in the palm of our hand. What we think, say and do from one minute to the next can have a dramatic impact on our own lives and the lives of those around us. At the end of the day we are all personally responsible for our own life – and to a great degree, it's up to us to choose what we do with it. Accepting full responsibility for your life is the starting-point in the 10-step process. When you accept that you create your own world, your life really can open up before you. At times it can be tempting to blame other people or circumstances for what happens, but when you do this essentially you're disempowering yourself, which doesn't really get you anywhere. As your coach, I want you to choose to accept responsibility for all that happens to you in your life from now on – good or bad, positive or negative. Whilst you can't determine the behaviour of those around you or influence natural disasters or acts of God, you *can* choose how you react to them. I want you to acknowledge that your behaviour is the result of your own choice.

☆ Can you remember a specific time in your life when you took full responsibility? What were the circumstances? How did you feel?

WHEN WENT 2 LONDON AGAINST EBODY. FELT WONDERFUL!

☆ What changes are you willing to make now to take more responsibility for your life going forward?

CHANGE JOD 9-5pm.
Move AUSTRALIA?

Develop a Strong Sense of Personal Integrity & Honesty

Life becomes significantly easier when you're able to live honestly with yourself. When you fully master this quality, few things can really threaten you. You'll find you have fewer problems and possess an innate sense of inner peace and calm. When you know and accept yourself for who you are as a person and are genuinely giving of your best, you don't have to waste your time and energy trying to be anything else.

Being 'in integrity' means not only accepting responsibility for your actions, but also being true to yourself, having self-respect and taking good care of all aspects of your physical, mental, emotional and spiritual being. Are you doing the best for yourself and your body? Are you stressed out? Are you eating and/or drinking too much? Are you running on adrenalin? Are you overlooking problems? Are you avoiding telling the truth? Are you not taking adequate time for yourself?

A person who is 'out of integrity' is like someone whose spine is out of alignment – their total being is unable to operate at its optimum capability. When your life is out of integrity, things tend to go wrong and you're highly likely to blame others. You'll know when you're out of integrity when there are significant gaps between what you say and what you do.

You can start to enhance your own personal integrity by identifying 10 areas of your life where you're not currently telling the full truth – either to yourself or others. List them and then write next to each one the actions you will take to address it and the date by which you will have completed them.

I'd like you to tackle two of these issues each week over the next month or so until you know you're living a fully authentic life.

1. People do not like me – So, why do they take time to talk to me then? They do!

2. I am not normal – I am, for sure

3. I am fine with my life

4. I want no help

> ☆ *The greatest discovery of my generation is that a human being can alter his life by altering his attitudes of mind!* ☆
>
> **William James**

Don't 'Should' on Yourself

When you're out of integrity and out of alignment with your own true self, it's likely you'll find yourself doing things because you feel others expect it of you rather than doing things because you really want to do them. This is where the 'shoulds' and 'oughts' come in. Coaches have a very useful phrase: 'Don't should on yourself.' In essence, if you say you 'should' or 'ought to' do something, unless you know it's something you genuinely need to do, the chances are the statement is coming from someone else's agenda and not from your own.

Be aware in your day-to-day life of how many times you say 'I should do this' or 'I should do that' – for example, do you ever say to yourself 'I should lose weight' or 'I should change jobs'? Stop and think. Ask yourself: 'Is this something I genuinely need or want to do?' I'm not suggesting you abdicate responsibility for things that it is necessary for you to do. We all have things in life that we don't particularly enjoy doing (housework or paperwork, for example), but we know we need to get them done. These are basic needs that you knuckle down and get on with. Equally, you may be required to take care of the needs of someone else (a sick relative perhaps), which is a question of facing up to your responsibilities. From a realistic viewpoint, I'd like you to be aware of your needs, responsibilities and wants and make choices accordingly. If your 'should' is neither a need nor a genuine responsibility nor a want, I suggest it is not a true expression of yourself and not appropriate for you to do!

> ☆ Be aware of your language over the next few days and take note of how many times you say 'should' and 'ought'. List your 10 most common 'shoulds' and 'oughts', decide whether they are things you genuinely need or want to do and if they are not, consider what you are going to do about them.

I actively encourage you to connect as much as you can with the real reasons why you do things. If something doesn't feel right to you, don't do it. For example, if you find yourself working extra hours each week, ask yourself, 'Is there a good reason for this? How is it serving me?' If the answer is that this is something you need to do, because you're being paid overtime and you need the extra money perhaps, or the project is important to you, your company, client or customer, and you will all benefit, then the justification is there. However, if the real reason you're working longer is because you feel you 'should' because everyone else does or you've just got into the habit, stop and ask yourself whether you can do this differently. Are you 'shoulding' on yourself? Would it serve you better to develop ways of becoming more effective and productive in fewer hours?

Your life will become more fulfilling when you eliminate any sense of obligation to things that don't really serve you. Do the things you want to for your highest good – it's your life!

Be Proactive

Being proactive means taking the initiative and not waiting for things to happen to you. People who are successful in life tend to be proactive – they are aware every day that the life they live is their own choice. It's not so much what happens to you in life that's important – it's what you do with what happens. Equally, it's not so much how you fall down that matters, but how you get up again!

As you embark on transforming your life, you'll encounter many choices and will start to become a real expert in making decisions. The more choices you make, the easier things will become and the freer you'll feel. Before you've finished reading this book, I want decision-making to be like falling off a log! But first, consider:

> ☆ What are the main factors that you think are limiting the choices you have in your life? *What people will think, too get dependant.*
>
> ☆ Taking these factors into account, what changes could you make to become more proactive? *Stop think what people will say. And also know that if I don't take any chance I will be dependant just beause of that!*

Adopt a Positive Attitude

Every second of every day we can choose how we view the world. Our own reality is held in place by our perceptions and our current state of awareness. So it goes without saying that the more positive your attitude, the more easily you'll be able to cope with transformation.

Is your cup half full or half empty? The moment you start to acknowledge that life is essentially 'good', your perceptions of the world automatically shift you into a new way of being. You may not be quite ready for this shift now, but if you are willing to open yourself up to the possibility, you could find a gradual sense of positivity creeping up on you as you transform your life.

When you start to adopt a more positive outlook on life, you still accept reality, but choose to live in a more fulfilling way. You find positive things start to happen to you and that you attract more positive people into your life.

> ☆ What evidence do you have now of positivity in your life?
>   List the three most positive elements of your current life.

There are various ways you can adopt a more positive mind-set. Some suggestions are appreciating and expressing gratitude for the good things in your life, and making sure you choose your words carefully, using positive, empowering language to express yourself and not undermining yourself with a negative inner dialogue or self-belief. Terms such as 'I can't' or 'It's impossible' set you up for failure before you even begin!

> ☆ What changes are you willing to make to become more positive
>   in your life?

Be Willing to Extend your Comfort Zones

It's not uncommon to fear change and the unknown. We're only human and it's human to suffer from a lack of nerve sometimes. As you work through this process

I would like you to accept your own humanness. Accept that it's alright to feel nervous, allow yourself to be comfortable with your 'discomfort', but then go beyond that and have the confidence to take perhaps the tiniest step towards the changes you want to make.

Making changes can result in successful or less successful outcomes. If you really want to transform your life you have to feel comfortable in accepting that sometimes things may not work out as you would like them to. However, don't forget, you'll learn from every action you take. As you go through the coaching process you'll stretch yourself, make a few mistakes along the way and learn from them. Once you accept that by living with uncertainty you will have the space to make the right choice, life becomes a lot easier. I want you to be willing to make mistakes and take steps into the unknown.

Trust your Intuition

Inner confidence and faith in yourself are valuable qualities and the more you can access them, the more readily you'll be able to manage the changes in your life. You can develop more of these characteristics if you pay attention to yourself and become more aware of your inner wisdom. I want you to make your intuition your ally, trust yourself and go with your 'gut' feelings.

How does your intuition speak to you? Do you receive information in words, do you get insights coming into your head or feelings in your body? If you're unfamiliar with accessing your intuition, ask yourself where you feel things in your body. If you have a decision to make, sit quietly and see where you feel something. The chances are you probably feel 'excitement' in one part of your body (maybe a fluttering sensation in your stomach, for example) and fear or foreboding in another area (your throat drying up perhaps?) You can use these feelings to interpret what your intuition is trying to tell you. Create the time and space to access your inner depths, be patient and allow yourself to discover your own answers when the time is right for you. Ask your intuition questions and pay attention to the answers. These might come to you as a quick flash of inspiration, an insight in a dream, a sense of 'knowing' in the pit of your stomach or perhaps a well-timed coincidence that endorses your own thoughts or makes sense to you in some way.

As your coach I want you to learn how to 'get out of your own way', to develop the ability to get out of your head and into your heart so you connect with your own inner wisdom on a regular basis. Getting out of your own way means putting your ego to one side and getting in touch with your own truth.

Often transformation begins with faith rather than fact. You need to have faith to trust your body's instincts, your heart's intuition and your mind's ability to work things out. But as you learn to step aside from your ego and learn to be really your-self, you make more room for truth and happiness.

☆ What actions can you take to access your own intuition.

Have Confidence & Act as though You're Already There

People with confidence tend to move their lives on fairly quickly. Confidence is a very sexy attribute. We'll be working on it more in Steps 4 and 9. For the time being I'd like you to become aware of how confident you feel. Even if you do not feel very con-fident now, acting as though you are already achieving what you want will propel you forwards in life. You'll be surprised how your confidence catches up with you!

☆ What do you think is stopping you from being more confident?

☆ What are you willing and able to do to overcome these obstacles?

☆ *Where the heart lies, let the brain lie also.'* ☆

Robert Browning

Picture your Results at the Beginning

One of the key principles of success is to know your outcome, what you want to achieve. It's only by understanding your objectives that you can work out the relevant strategy to achieve them. Also, knowing your desired outcome helps to keep you on track when you start to focus on the details.

As you start your transformation process I'd like you to be clear about what you want to achieve. To help you, take a look at the following questions:

☆ How, specifically, will you know that your time spent following the 10-step process will have been worthwhile? What would have *happened* in your life?

☆ If there was one important *change* that you could make in the next three months, what would it be?

☆ Is there something that you need to *start* (or *stop*) doing that would have a significant impact on your life?

☆ If you could give this next phase of your life transformation an overall *theme*, what would it be? (Examples could include 'Creating Space for Me', 'Developing a Life I Love', 'Moving my Business to the Next Level', 'Attracting my Ideal Life Partner' and so on.)

My theme is:

☆ List three *specific goals* you want to achieve over the next *year*.

☆ List three *specific goals* you want to achieve in the next *three months*.

☆ Looking at your life now, what's the *biggest opportunity* that you're not taking full advantage of?

☆ What's getting *in the way* of you having the life you really want?

Key Insights Gained from Step 1

☆
☆
☆

Quick Wins Gained from Step 1

☆
☆
☆

The Action Steps I Will Now Take

Action   Deadline date

☆   ☆
☆   ☆
☆   ☆

Real Results

(To maintain confidentiality, names have been changed.)

Martin *IT director, single, 40s*

Martin was in a fast-paced, financially rewarding career, but was feeling run down and demotivated. Successful on the outside, he felt empty on the inside. He wanted to find a sense of satisfaction and achievement in his life, but didn't know where to start.

The Value of Coaching

To help Martin see the bigger picture of his life, restore his integrity so he had a clear idea of what he wanted to do rather than what he felt he 'should' do, and clarify his priorities, so he could move forwards on his own terms.

☆ **Life Perspective Questions**

These made Martin realize how he'd always been focused on his work and bank balance and had lost sight of other things in life. He realized that if money wasn't an issue for him, he'd start studying a language and learning new skills. Also, he loved photography and would like to learn more about it and maybe become a professional photographer. He was surprised by his own answers and realized he wanted to express his buried creativity.

☆ **The Wheel of Life**

Martin's wheel was totally out of balance, with high scores for money and career and low scores for everything else. This was a clear indication that he'd been burying his head in the sand for too long. No wonder he felt empty. I challenged him to leave work earlier several days a week and plan more personal time for himself.

☆ Set Yourself Up for Success

Martin acknowledged he was out of alignment, feeling stressed, drinking too much and running on adrenalin. He realized he was living his life according to quite a few 'shoulds', which were mostly based around earning money, of which he already had reserves. I challenged him to think about what he 'wanted' to do instead. His list of 'wants' included doing more photography, learning to cook and to speak French, playing the stock market and socializing more.

Real Results

Martin started addressing his health and well-being, joined a gym and scheduled in sessions three times per week, with the result that he started to feel more energetic. His physical environment was uninspiring and he'd ignored his home, so he employed a cleaner and his sister-in-law agreed to help him clear out his kitchen, make new curtains and give the place a make-over. This started to get him motivated. He also decided to convert the spare room into an office, so he could spend fewer hours at work. He bought a computer and developed a power-base at home. He looked at improving his social life, planned a dinner party once a month and joined a dating agency to meet new people.

"I now have a five-year plan that involves leaving work, undertaking various streams of education that will include doing an MSc and an MBA and studying maths and a foreign language and culminate in developing a business plan and doing a PhD. Even if I do not actually complete all these things I still know that the journey will lead to a rewarding change to my life. I feel more positive about life.

Short-term, I have been on a photography holiday, am actively developing photography as a hobby and have framed some prints to decorate my home. My social life is pretty active now and I'm fitter, more energetic and healthier than I've been for years."

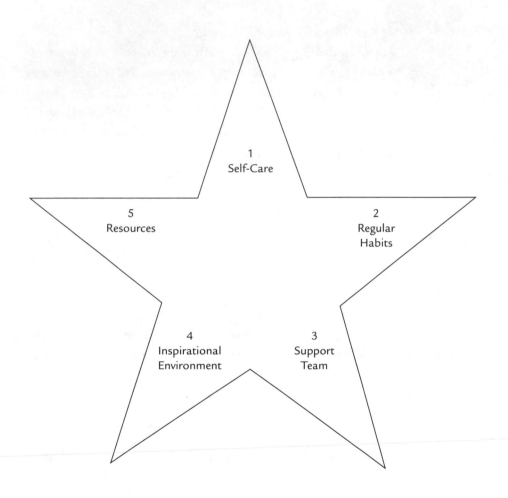

1
Self-Care

5
Resources

2
Regular
Habits

4
Inspirational
Environment

3
Support
Team

build the
right
foundations

☆ *Luck is when preparedness*

meets opportunity. ☆

Earl Nightingale

Overview

If you want to transform your life and turn your dreams into reality, it goes without saying that you need to develop the right foundations first. A launch pad requires strong foundations from which a rocket can reach into the sky. My role as your coach is to ensure that you have the strongest foundations possible on which to build your life.

To set yourself up for success, I want you to make sure you're taking the best possible care of yourself. As you work through Step 2 you'll be encouraged to integrate regular habits into your life and to build a strong support framework and power base.

You may be tempted to charge ahead with goals and plans, but the time you spend on creating your foundations is an investment that will pay off for the rest of your life.

When you've completed this step:

☆ You'll be taking exceptional care of your physical, mental and emotional well-being.

☆ You'll have established regular habits to support you for the rest of your life.

☆ You'll have identified a team of people to support you as you transform your life.

☆ You'll have created an inspirational environment and a strong base to work from.

☆ You'll have set up invaluable systems and resources to bring out your best.

Personal Reward for Completing Step 2

☆ Write down here how you will reward yourself when you have completed Step 2:

Quick Transformation Quiz

Answer the questions below by ticking the appropriate box and calculating your score as follows:
2 points = Yes/Agree/Not Applicable, 1 point = Agree sometimes, 0 point = No/Disagree

		YES	SOMETIMES	NO
1	My body is in good shape, I'm happy with my weight and I exercise regularly.	❏	❏	❏
2	I eat plenty of healthy food for sustenance and pleasure but not for emotional comfort.	❏	❏	❏
3	I reduce stress daily by relaxing or meditating, taking a bath, walking, etc.	❏	❏	❏
4	I have created a tranquil, harmonious home.	❏	❏	❏
5	I am not abusing my body with too much alcohol and caffeine (coffee, tea chocolate, fizzy drinks) or drugs.	❏	❏	❏
6	I only wear clothes that make me feel good.	❏	❏	❏
7	I have had a physical examination within the last three years and my cholesterol and blood pressure are at a healthy level.	❏	❏	❏
8	I don't smoke or misuse prescribed medication.	❏	❏	❏
9	I visit my dentist and hygienist regularly and my teeth and gums are healthy.	❏	❏	❏
10	I get my eyes tested regularly.	❏	❏	❏
11	I have lots of energy and vitality.	❏	❏	❏
12	I have as much sleep as I need to function happily.	❏	❏	❏
13	I have things to look forward to and smile and laugh out loud every day.	❏	❏	❏
14	I have a haircut that makes me feel great.	❏	❏	❏

15   I have regular breaks, take evenings and weekends off and use my holiday allotment for pure relaxation (no chores). ❏ ❏ ❏

16   My home is filled with the furniture, décor, art and music that I love. ❏ ❏ ❏

17   I have a circle of close friends and family who love and appreciate me for who I truly am. ❏ ❏ ❏

18   I like the geographical area in which I live/work. ❏ ❏ ❏

19   I minimize the time I spend with people who drain me or try to change me. ❏ ❏ ❏

20   I receive plenty of love from people around me and tell them how they can support and help me. ❏ ❏ ❏

Initial Score ❏ **Score on Completion of Step 2** ❏

Final Score on Completion of Book ❏

☆ *Motivation is like food for the brain. You cannot get enough in one sitting. It needs continual and regular refills.* ☆

Peter Davies

Take the Best Care of Yourself

If you want to transform your life, you need to transform yourself first. To do this, it's important to make your own self-care your number one priority.

I'd like to make a distinction here between self-care and being selfish, as these two terms are quite different. Some people feel uncomfortable about putting their own self-care first, thinking it a very selfish way of behaving. From a coaching point of view, self-care is a 'self-ful' activity, not a 'self-ish' one. The more you work on yourself, invest in yourself, take care of yourself and fill your own cup, the more you have to give others. I actually believe it's selfish *not* to take care of yourself first. When you neglect yourself you're running on empty tanks, which drains energy from other people rather than supports them. Remember, you can't give what you don't have, so unless you love and nurture yourself first, you won't be able to give these gifts to others.

How did you score your health and well-being on the Wheel of Life in Step 1? How did you score on the Transformation Quiz? You've probably already gained a few clues as how you can take better care of yourself.

> ☆ List the ways you're currently taking care of yourself.
> What are you doing to put yourself first?

Surprisingly few of us are as kind to ourselves as we'd like to be. Late nights, excessive eating, drinking, smoking and other bad habits don't do you any favours. I challenge you to take action *now* to take the best possible care of yourself – for a start, why not book yourself in for a massage, spend more time with friends, have a fabulous haircut or do more of something you really enjoy?

Are You Getting Sufficient Sleep?

A common issue I address with clients is one of adequate sleep. These days few of us get as much sleep as we really need to operate at our best. Whether you're someone who needs eight hours each night or someone who can function quite happily on only six hours is for you to decide. Why not track the number of hours sleep you are actually getting over the next week and compare it with the number of hours you know you really need? Do you need to make any changes here? I would like you to put a system in place to ensure that you have a regular pattern of perfect sleep for you. I challenge you to go to bed no later than 10 p.m. at least one night per week!

☆ My ideal sleep pattern is:

Eating Well

If you want to lead a healthy, energetic life, eating well goes without saying. Ensure you nourish your body with adequate nutrients, cut down on fat, junk foods, alcohol and caffeine and drink plenty of water. You might decide your body needs an occasional 'de-tox' to really enhance your well-being and sense of self.

☆ What specific changes are you willing to make to improve your diet and enhance your vitality?

Regular Exercise

Regular exercise is an essential ingredient for a healthy life. I challenge you to commit to at least 30 minutes of exercise you enjoy three or four times a week. If you have young children and find it difficult to get out of the house, use an exercise video, go out walking and look for ways you can become more active in your everyday life. If you work long hours and have a sedentary lifestyle, exercise is crucial for you. Playing a sport might be ideal for you – maybe golf, tennis or badminton – or perhaps swimming or yoga would suit you better. There is a wide range of exercise options. Select the activities that appeal to you the most, decide how often you want to do them and plan them into your life.

Enjoying sunshine and fresh air and breathing deeply are also key elements to enhance your vitality. Take regular walks and spend time outside in nature to restore yourself.

☆ What do you want your own personal exercise regime to look like? Write down specific activities, detailing when, where and how often you'll be doing them.

Health Checks

I know these can be easy to overlook, but they are an important way of helping you to identify any possible problems at an early stage, so you can nip them in the bud. Are you scheduling regular visits to the dentist, doctor, optician, nutritionist and/or other appropriate professionals?

Your Image and Appearance

Your appearance is a reflection to the outside world of the inner you and the extent to which you value yourself. If you are looking and feeling great, you will be exuding confidence, energy and vitality as you go about your daily life. Are your clothes, shoes and accessories doing you justice? Clear out or give away anything that doesn't suit you or make you feel good.

I want you to develop your own sense of personal style. If you want to try a cost-effective way of changing your clothes, why not visit a dress agency and experiment with a few quality second-hand items? You might want to visit an image consultant or get a free make-up lesson at a cosmetics counter to get ideas. Wear the colours and styles that bring out your best. The same goes for your hair, make-up and skin-care – making the most of your own natural features will make you feel better about yourself.

☆ What are you willing to do to enhance your appearance?

Interests, Fun and Inspiration

These are an important part of your self-care and a fabulous way of nurturing your soul. I want you to ensure you're sprinkling plenty of music, humour, dance, interests and hobbies over your life so you have something to look forward to every day. It goes without saying that the more you fill your life with things you enjoy – big or small – the greater your sense of contentment will be.

What are the things that give you a real sense of joy? Perhaps for you it's spending quality time with your children or sleeping on freshly laundered bedding, playing tennis or having fresh flowers and candles in your home.

> ☆ What changes do you want to make to sprinkle more fun
> and inspiration over your life?

Regular Breaks

Time to relax, recharge and re-energize is crucial to looking after yourself well. Taking quick five-minute breaks during your day or a few minutes out of your regular schedule to do something for yourself is the perfect antidote to a busy day. The occasional long weekend break and proper holidays during the year will also help to keep you on top form.

> ☆ What are you doing to ensure you take quality time to rest,
> relax and recharge?

> ☆ What holiday plans are you going to make for the next 12 months?

> ☆ In summary, what are the three things you could start to do now
> that would have the biggest impact on yourself physically, mentally
> and emotionally during this next phase of your life?

Establish your Regular Habits

One of the best ways to start integrating life-enhancing activities into your day-to-day life is to establish regular habits – things you agree to do daily, weekly or monthly for the foreseeable future.

These habits can be small, but if carried out on a regular basis will greatly enhance your life. Possible suggestions include exercising for at least 20 minutes every day (whether that's a brisk walk or a workout in the gym is entirely up to you!), having at least seven to eight hours sleep every night, drinking a couple of litres of water a day, having a real laugh with someone each day, having a fortnightly massage, making three new work contacts each week, returning phone calls immediately, reading an inspirational poem or smiling at a stranger at least once a day.

Think about the habits you want to take up that will support you in being the person you want to be, living the life you really want.

Keep a Daily Inspiration Journal

As one of your regular habits, I actively encourage you to maintain a daily inspiration journal. Keeping a diary or journal to record your thoughts, insights, intuitive ideas and actions as your new life unfolds will support you profoundly during your transformation process. Not only will it help you to clarify your thoughts and build your confidence in yourself, but it will also serve as a very interesting memento to refer back to from time to time, so you really can see how far you've progressed!

Updating your daily inspiration journal will require self-discipline at first, but please persist. Once you get into the routine of making your daily entries, you'll find the five or ten minutes it takes will greatly enhance your life. Treat yourself to a notebook or diary that inspires you and start writing today!

Some people find it beneficial to make entries in their journal briefly twice a day, in the morning and at night. You might prefer to choose just one of these times.

You might include your thoughts on the following:

> ☆ things about the day that make you feel happy/confident and/or excited

> ☆ things that you appreciate, are proud of or are committed to doing

> ☆ people and things in the day that you love and why

> ☆ things that may not be quite right but which you have plans to change

> ☆ things you have learned in the day or that have helped you to develop in some way

If you want to keep your inspiration journal really focused, why not write down your top three 'big wins' each day – the three key things that have been the highlights of your day?

Once you become disciplined about keeping your journal you'll find yourself gaining a heightened sense of awareness of what makes you happy and will become more appreciative of some of the simple things in your life. The real benefits come when you start to take action on your discoveries by doing more of the things you enjoy and less of those you don't! Try to keep a daily inspiration journal for the next month and see how it enhances your life! Remember, gratitude is the attitude which determines your altitude!

White Space

An incredibly useful habit many of my clients derive great benefit from is creating 15 minutes of 'white space' each day. What I mean by 'white space' is totally silent time when you simply do nothing, just quieten your mind and be still for 15 minutes. You might like to sit quietly or even meditate. Whatever you do, just allowing yourself some quiet time gives you the opportunity to get in touch with your inner self. If you find the prospect of 15 minutes a little daunting, start with just five minutes of silence and gradually build up. Or do more if it works for you! You may be surprised how refreshed and inspired you feel afterwards.

Some people find doing this first thing in the morning is the perfect way of setting up the day, while for others it may be after lunch or last thing at night.

It goes without saying that the more you take care of yourself, the stronger your own power base becomes. I'm sure you know theoretically what's good for you, but your real challenge is to take action and integrate these things into your life.

> ☆ List your own 10 *regular habits* and how often
> you'll do them.

Start tomorrow. You'll be amazed how by paying attention to the little details in life, things start to move on a much bigger scale!

☆ *Though we travel the world over*

to find the beautiful, we must carry

it within us, or we find it not. ☆

Ralph Waldo Emerson

Build your Empowering Support Team

I have already stressed the importance of surrounding yourself with key people to support you and to hold you accountable for your actions. I trust that you're already benefiting from their help? There are undoubtedly times in your life when it's useful to spend time alone and to work things through for yourself. However, no matter how self-sufficient you are, there are also many occasions when your life can be significantly enhanced by the support of others.

Surround yourself with people who can help you take your life onto the next level – both an 'inner' and an 'outer' team. 'Inner' team members are a few key people you have relatively close contact with, see and speak to regularly and know are consistently there for you. Your 'outer' team members are those people who are more on the periphery of your life. You don't necessarily have direct access to them – they can be role models you admire from afar or useful contacts you touch base with every once in a while.

Build your Inner Team

You'll probably find it useful to divide your inner team members into two key categories: 'spark people' and 'fundamental support people'.

Spark People

Spark people are those who do just that – they spark you off with new ideas, they inspire you, challenge you, stretch you and encourage you to be all you can be and more. These people play an essential role in your own growth.

☆ Who has been a spark person for you in your life? Why and how did they achieve that?

☆ Who do you want to invite onto your spark team for the next phase of your life?

Fundamental Support People

Fundamental support people are those you connect with in your inner circle of friends, family and associates who you know you can totally rely on to be there to support you as you move your life forwards.

> ☆ Who has been a fundamental support for you in your life?
> Why and how did they achieve this? What specifically is it
> about them that you valued?

> ☆ Who do you want to invite onto your fundamental support
> team to help move you forward with the next phase of your life?

> ☆ If you could learn from anyone, who would be your mentor
> or guide? Why?

Once you've identified your inner team, tell each person individually how they can help you most and really acknowledge them for the role they are about to play in your life.

Build your Outer Team

Now it's time to identify those people who are on the periphery of your life but nevertheless will have a positive impact on you as you move forward. Whether they are role models or people in your network, the chances are they'll represent something important to you and will inspire you or become useful contacts you may wish to call upon in your new life.

Identify your Role Models

A powerful way of enhancing your own sense of self is to gain inspiration from others around you. Learning from role models can be a great way of developing yourself quickly. Be aware of people who impress you for a particular reason, ask yourself why and what you can learn from this particular person. What is it about them that you admire? Can you modify what they do to suit your own personality? You may find it useful to read autobiographies of successful people, listen to tapes, go to workshops – do whatever will support and inspire you.

Can you identify three role models, people who inspire you, who you can learn from and feel motivated by?

☆ My three role models are:
☆ I admire them because:
☆ The qualities I would like to emulate are:
☆ I will do this by:

The more you surround yourself with successful, inspirational people, the more you'll learn and the greater the likelihood that some of it may rub off on you!

Strengthen your Network

Can you identify the key people in your network who can help you take your life to the next level? Are you making the most of your relationships with them? Is there more you can do to develop and nurture those relationships? Who are the top three people in your wider environment who inspire and motivate you? Are you spending sufficient time with them? They could help catapult you to the top of your field!

☆ My top three catapults:

Useful Contacts

As background support to enhance your overall life, I want you to build a comprehensive address book of useful contacts for you to call on when needed. The following list will provide you with suggestions which I'm sure you can modify to suit your own needs. Once you've completed your own contact list, you'll have comprehensive details of a variety of support people to help you in the next phase of your life. Why not spend the next 10 days filling in as many of the contact details as you can? You might want to share the list with friends and swap useful contacts between you!

Contact	Number	Name
Accountant/Bookkeeper	....	
Banker	....	
Beautician	....	
Car care/garage	....	
Caterer	....	
Child care/Babysitter	....	
Chiropractor	....	
Complementary therapist/	....	
Nutritionist/Homoeopath	....	
Computer servicer	....	
Dentist	....	
Doctor	....	
Dressmaker/tailor	....	
Electrician	....	
Feng shui consultant	....	
Financial adviser	....	
Hairdresser	....	
Handyman/woman	....	
Healthy food delivery	....	
Housekeeper/cleaner	....	
Image consultant	....	
Insurance expert	....	
Interior designer/decorator	....	
Lifecoach	....	
Massage therapist/Physiotherapist	....	
Optician	....	
Personal trainer	....	
Plumber	....	
Solicitor	....	
Stockbroker	....	
Vet	....	

Create an Inspirational Environment

Developing an inspirational environment, both at home and at work, is a key element of your launch pad. I want you to create a tranquil, harmonious home as one of the cornerstones of your life. If the space you inhabit has a positive atmosphere, you're more likely to be in a position to operate at your best.

Do you like the area where you live? Do you like the area where you work? If it's not ideal, what can you do to make the best of it? Is your home somewhere you can relax and recharge? Does it suit your preferred lifestyle? Are you happy with the lay-out, the furniture, the décor?

Sometimes small changes at home – painting a wall, putting a candle in the bedroom, changing the lighting, adding shelving, fresh flowers, music, pictures – can make a big difference. At work, adding plants and making sure you have a clear desk and tidy files can give you more energy to be productive. Think what you can do to improve your own space.

☆ What changes do you want to make to your home?

☆ What changes do you want to make to the area where you work?

☆ *How many cares one loses when one decides not to be something, but [instead] someone.* ☆

Coco Chanel

5 Identify Physical Resources to Support You

The final element in developing your foundations is ensuring you have the right physical resources around you to operate at your best. What do you need to enhance your life – tools, machinery, electrical equipment, lighting, a computer, a dishwasher, fridge-freezer, furniture, car, music centre?

☆ What resources are you missing that would enhance your home life?

☆ What resources are you missing that would enhance your work life?

☆ What systems do you need to put in place to help you operate at your best?

☆ What resources can you surround yourself with to optimize your performance, productivity and sense of fulfilment?

☆ What else would be useful to you (information, books, life-skills, knowledge, etc)?

☆ *When we truly care for ourselves it becomes possible to care more profoundly about other people.* ☆

Edith Le Shen

Key Insights Gained from Step 2

☆

☆

☆

Quick Wins Gained from Step 2

☆

☆

☆

The Action Steps I Will Now Take

Action   Deadline date

☆   ☆

☆   ☆

☆   ☆

Real Results

Jane *Self-employed, separated mother of two, 40s*

Jane was exhausted, stressed and confused. She was going through a messy separation, had financial worries and had left her job to go freelance. She was questioning her career direction and feeling on a downward spiral and unproductive. Her health was not as good as she wanted it to be and she was unsure what to do next.

The Value of Coaching

To help Jane build the right foundations on which to base her life, get her to take better care of herself (which would ultimately benefit her children), develop strong support systems and gain a clear sense of direction.

☆ **Self-Care**

Jane immediately realized she was taking very little care of herself – eating on the run, having little sleep or exercise and no holidays. She had never even considered her own needs – she thought putting herself first was being selfish. Then she realized that by not taking care of herself she had become a 'shell' of a person, constantly tired, snappy with the children and unproductive in her work. Jane worked from home and found it very difficult to get motivated. She didn't have another project lined up when her current one finished and so was worrying about money and feeling short-tempered. For her, the first step was to look at her diet, eat more fresh food and drink more water. She also took up yoga and walking the dog.

☆ **Sleep**

The first real breakthrough was getting Jane to address her lack of sleep. She was going to bed at one or two in the morning, waking up in the middle of the night worrying, falling back to sleep around six, feeling too tired to get up in the morning, then rushing around and starting every day off badly. I challenged her to start logging her sleep pattern. Helping Jane to establish a clear awareness of her reality made her take responsibility for herself. Even she was surprised by how little real sleep she was having. She accepted my challenge of going to bed before 11 p.m. at least three nights a week and we gradually built it up to five nights. I also challenged her to get up no later than 7.30 a.m. on weekdays. She monitored her progress and even drew a graph to show the number of hours she slept. This may sound silly, but to Jane, the more attention she paid to sleeping, the better she found she became. Once she was sleeping for at least seven quality hours a night, her life started to move forward in leaps and bounds.

☆ Regular Habits

Jane established 10 regular habits for her life, sleep being the number one priority, and we moved on from there. She started to keep a daily inspiration journal to monitor her progress and would e-mail me copies, so she knew there was a purpose to it all. Weeks later she found it really useful to look back over her journal and see how she was gradually changing her life and moving out of the rut.

☆ Support Team

Jane was amazed to realize she'd existed for the last few years without any obvious support from others! At first she was reluctant to select three support people, but when she did and told them she was in the process of transforming her life, they were only too happy to help. In return they found they learned a lot in the process and benefited from some of the assignments Jane undertook.

Real Results

Jane had more space, time and energy to focus on her two most important priorities: her sons and her work. They all went on holiday together for the first time in ages, started to take trips to the cinema and go together for walks with the dog. As she had more energy, Jane started to network more, meet new people and her new sense of direction and energy made her very attractive to those around her. She landed a fabulous new work assignment in Malawi and her life really started to take off. She is now supporting her sons through their GCSEs and 'A' levels and is doing research work from home for the time being, with talk of work in Kosovo when the boys finish their exams. Her life has become exciting. Together we developed a clear plan of where she's going and have mapped out small steps to take her there. She is in the flow of her life and enjoying every minute of it!

"Coaching re-introduced the idea of excellence, success, striving for the highest goal, realizing my potential. . . This is feasible now because of the strong foundation and the continuing idea of acceptance, compassion, realism, etc. Before, I didn't have a strong foundation, so my strivings for success were rattling around on a flimsy base.

Regular Habits is an exercise which I would single out as particularly useful. It helped me to overcome my problem with mornings and continues to be very helpful as I further refine my daily routing to make myself more efficient and to make life easier and more enjoyable. The Habits worked well for me because it reminded me how important the little day-to-day rituals and routines are — they underpin everything else and have a big influence on how together you are. It's easy to underestimate them. It can also be embarrassing to confront the fact that, at the age of (in my case) 42, I had not got sorted the question of how to start my day. Coaching makes it alright to be explicit about this and to re-evaluate the whole question of habits and routines to see how they are either supporting or jeopardizing what you want to achieve."

☆ ***So much of what you are not is because you are literally standing in your own way of becoming.*** ☆

Lee Buscaglia

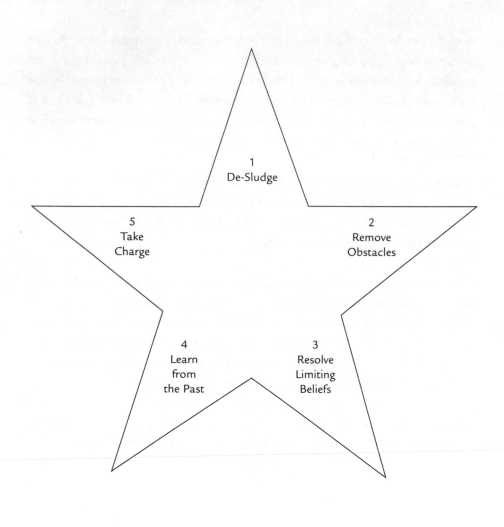

spring
clean
your **life**

☆ *Maintaining a complicated life is*

a great way to avoid changing it. ☆

Elaine St. James

Overview

By now you've probably already started to make some of the subtle changes needed to enhance your life. This next step is crucial in clearing your path ahead. If you want to make fundamental changes in your life you need to have enough space and time to do so. We're all so busy these days that we rarely take the opportunity to sit down quietly and look at things clearly. Clarity often only comes after we've given our lives a bit of a 'spring clean'.

If you liken yourself to a computer, the chances are your hard drive is already overloaded and you have relatively little free space for anything new. As you work through this step you'll be clearing out your hard drive and creating more physical, mental and emotional space for the next phase of your life. Your future will move in faster once you have space for it!

As well as giving your life a thorough spring clean, you'll be identifying the fundamental issues that may be holding you back. I will be supporting you in addressing and overcoming any obstacles that could disrupt the flow of your transformation. I want you to embark on the next phase of your life with no weeds in your garden!

When you've completed this step:

> ☆ You'll have addressed many of the energy-draining niggles you've been putting up with in your life.

> ☆ You'll have de-cluttered your home and work environment.

> ☆ You'll have worked through any obstacles that could block your way ahead.

> ☆ You'll have started to overcome your limiting beliefs and to turn your problems into opportunities.

☆ You'll be learning from your past experiences.

☆ You'll have freed up more energy to concentrate on the more important things in life.

☆ You'll feel more in charge of empowering yourself.

Personal Reward for Completing Step 3

☆ Write down here how you will reward yourself when you have completed Step 3:

Quick Transformation Quiz

Answer the questions below by ticking the appropriate box and calculating your score as follows:

2 points = Yes/Agree/Not Applicable, 1 point = Agree sometimes, 0 point = No/Disagree

		YES	SOMETIMES	NO
1	My home and work environments are de-cluttered and inspiring.	❏	❏	❏
2	My wardrobe and drawers are well organized and my clothes are cleaned and ironed.	❏	❏	❏
3	My paperwork, correspondence and receipts are filed away neatly.	❏	❏	❏
4	I am not putting up with anything in my home or work environment that niggles or annoys me.	❏	❏	❏
5	I don't have a lot of things hanging in the air, unfinished projects, business matters or other items.	❏	❏	❏
6	I have plenty of light, heat and fresh air around me.	❏	❏	❏
7	My equipment and appliances all work well.	❏	❏	❏
8	My plants and animals are flourishing.	❏	❏	❏

		YES	SOMETIMES	NO
9	My car is in good condition and is always reliable.	❏	❏	❏
10	My home and/or office is cleaned weekly and there's nothing in my environment that harms me.	❏	❏	❏
11	I don't overload my life with too much television, radio and newspapers.	❏	❏	❏
12	I have streamlined my life and things run smoothly.	❏	❏	❏
13	I am taking action on key lessons from my past experiences.	❏	❏	❏
14	I have let go of people and relationships that drag me down or have a negative influence over me.	❏	❏	❏
15	I have spring cleaned my emotional life and am not hanging on to people from my past.	❏	❏	❏
16	I don't gossip about others, judge or excessively criticize other people.	❏	❏	❏
17	I am aware of any limiting beliefs that are holding me back and am taking action to resolve them.	❏	❏	❏
18	I have forgiven those who have hurt me, inadvertently or not.	❏	❏	❏
19	There is no one in my life who I would feel uncomfortable or dread bumping into.	❏	❏	❏
20	I regularly tell those closest to me that I love them.	❏	❏	❏

Initial Score ❏ **Score on Completion of Step 3** ❏

Final Score on Completion of Book ❏

☆ *As we are liberated from our own fear, our presence automatically liberates others.* ☆

Marianne Williamson

De-Sludge your Life

We all have a certain amount of 'sludge' in our lives – issues, people and beliefs that block us, slow us down or drain our energy. We put up with clutter, niggly unfinished tasks and 'less than ideal' situations that divert us from the important things in life. If you want to be clear about your future, you need to get rid of as much of this 'sludge' as possible.

What are the niggles, big and small, in your life at this moment? Maybe you haven't really noticed until now all the little annoying things that are holding you back. We tolerate so many things unnecessarily. A negative friend, a faulty vacuum cleaner, a freezer that's too small, a photocopier that doesn't work properly, a pile of ironing, unfinished paperwork, a wilting plant, a dirty car, a client who wears us down – the list is endless!

☆ Make a list of the top 10 things that you're putting up with.

☆ Select two of these, address them and eliminate them by the end of this week.

Revisit your list and put a date by the side of each issue to confirm when you will have resolved it. Gradually, one by one, work at eliminating them. You'll find this process is ongoing. As you address certain niggles, new ones may crop up. An effective way of managing this is to develop a system for keeping on top of things. Perhaps you can set aside a specific time each week to tackle niggles and agree areas of responsibility with the people around you at home and/or work.

As you start to get rid of things you've been putting up with, you'll feel lighter and have more energy. The more actions you take, the more positive the space around you will become and the clearer your path ahead will appear!

Remove your Energy Drains

A major benefit in spring cleaning your life is the boost it provides to your energy flow. Successful people have more than enough energy – mental, physical and emotional – to carry their ideas and projects through to completion. Their energy visibly flows through them and can be contagious, captivating others and sweeping them along as things get done in double-quick time. To optimize your energy flow, you need to minimize your energy drains and maximize the energy coming into your life.

Clutter drains you of energy, so sort everything out, decide what to keep, throw out, give away, sell or store. Get rid of anything you don't absolutely need or haven't used in the last 12 months. Assign a home to everything you wish to keep and get organized to prevent the build up from occurring again. De-junk your entire life – cut down on TV, newspapers and information overload. Cancel subscriptions to publications you don't have the time to read. Limit your Internet access. Cut down on alcohol and junk food. Detox your body and your mind and blitz your environment. Keep asking yourself, 'What else can I do to simplify my life?'

> ☆ Is there anything draining your energy at this moment?
> If anything has escaped from your previous list, write it
> down now, together with a plan for eliminating it:

What Can You Say 'No' to in your Life?

'No' is an extremely powerful word which, in the early stages of transforming your life, can be most useful. The lifecoaching process itself encourages you to be positive and proactive. But often before you can do this you need to learn to say 'no' to anything or anyone that drains your energy and is not in your best interests.

In this busy world, where we're all encouraged to be upbeat and positive and to say 'yes' to life, many of us find it extremely difficult to say 'no'. If you're someone who is always chasing around after others, it's highly likely that you need to learn to say 'no' a lot more than you currently do. If something isn't enhancing your life, ask yourself why you're doing it. Is it worthwhile? Has it outlived its purpose in your life? If you don't have a very good reason for something, just say 'no' to it!

If you find it difficult, practise. Stand in front of a mirror and let your mouth form the word 'no'. Next time you're faced with a request, buy yourself time by saying, 'Can I think about it?'

Someone once said to me, 'If you never say "no", then what is your "yes" worth?' If you think about this for a minute, by saying 'no', what you are doing is creating the space for your 'yes' to really mean something.

Make the things you say 'yes' to those that you can give your all to – those times when you can really help someone or those things that give you and others a great deal of pleasure. Let someone else do whatever it is you really want to say 'no' to!

> ☆ List your top 10 'no's – things you will eliminate from your life in
> order to ease your transformation.
> 'I will no longer...'

☆ *Saying yes and no clearly builds confidence and rids us of the misconception that we are powerless.* ☆

Marsha Sinetar

Identify & Overcome any Obstacles

The chances are you probably have a few obstacles blocking the way between where you are now and where you want to be. Once you become more aware of these, you can start to develop ways of overcoming them.

The obstacles can either be internal or external. Internal obstacles are thoughts, feelings and ways of behaving that prevent you from reaching your full potential. External obstacles are outside issues that have an impact on your life. Take a look at the following threats and tick the ones that are likely to influence you or become an obstacle to your success:

Internal

Negative habits/attitudes
Procrastination
Fear
Low self-confidence
Perfectionism
Failure
Stress
Poor time management
Loneliness
Resistance to change
Limiting self-beliefs
Political change
Racism
Sexism

External

Money
Loss of your job
Divorce
Recession
Ageing parents
Dysfunctional family
Inflation
TV and media
Ageism
Addictions
Fear of success
Depression
Hopelessness

☆ *Surmounting difficulty is the crucible that forms character.* ☆

Anthony Robins

Rank them in order of importance – which ones have the greatest significance for you? Think of ways of addressing them one by one. What resources are available to you? Is there anyone in your support group who can help?

To give you added impetus to blast through your blocks, you might find it useful to gain a sense of perspective by asking yourself the following question:

> ☆ **Where is the pain for me in not transforming my life? What is it costing me to stay where I am?**

When you take responsibility and believe you can change, you will.

If you're having a problem with this, sit quietly and fast-forward your life to 10 years from now. Put yourself in the shoes of the future you. What advice would the future you give to the present you?

3 Resolve your Limiting Beliefs

We wouldn't be human if we didn't hold beliefs. Many are ingrained in us from a young age and become our reality without us even realizing it. Beliefs such as 'Life is a struggle' and 'You have to work hard to earn money' are very common.

If you're finding it difficult to make the progress you want, the chances are it is probably your beliefs that are holding you back in some way. They may be negative phrases you often find yourself repeating in your head. Time and again in my life-coaching sessions I come across a whole series of limiting beliefs such as 'I'm not good enough', 'Things like that don't happen to me', 'I'm too short/fat/stupid to succeed', 'I don't have the right skills for that role', 'My boss knows best', etc.

If you want to transform your life, becoming aware of the beliefs you hold is an important start. Understanding why you hold the beliefs you do and acknowledging the evidence to support them is the second stage. The next step is about turning limiting beliefs into empowering ones. Stage four is about finding the evidence to support the empowering beliefs. The final step involves implementing the empowering beliefs into your everyday life.

☆ What are your limiting beliefs?

☆ Which one do you think has the most influence over you?

☆ Why do you hold this belief? What evidence do you have to prove that it is true?

☆ What evidence do you have to prove to yourself that this belief is *not necessarily* true?

☆ What would be a more positive, empowering belief that could replace your old belief?

☆ What evidence do you have to support your new empowering belief?

☆ What are you willing to do differently to integrate this new empowering belief into your life transformation?

☆ What has to happen for you to feel in charge and able to overcome any blocks or limiting beliefs?

☆ *To conquer fear is the beginning of wisdom.* ☆

Bertrand Russell

Learn from your Past

When you fully spring clean your life, an important area to address is that of issues from the past, especially those left over from any difficult times. As we grow and experience life, we all have our fair share of these and it may be during our darkest moments that we learn some of our most valuable lessons. But sometimes issues from the past hang around and become recurring patterns. In order to move on, you need to do something about them! Clearing up old issues and learning from past mistakes or disappointments can give you much firmer foundations for your future.

☆ What has your attention been drawn to during the more difficult periods of your life?

☆ What are the hardest lessons you've had to learn?

☆ Is there a problem or theme that rears its head time and time again?

☆ If you keep repeating the same pattern, why do you think this is so?

☆ Do you care enough about it to do something about it once and for all? If so, what will you do?

Accept that the Present is Perfect

Everything happens to us for a reason and every person comes into our lives to teach us something. Ask yourself what you have learned from each difficult experience in your life. What have been your most valuable lessons? What you have learned in the past has set the scene for the present – and whatever you're experiencing at this very moment is perfectly appropriate to your need to grow.

☆ What have been the three most valuable lessons in your life and what have you learned from them?

5 ☆ Take Charge and Empower Yourself

Energy Boosters

Once your energy blocks, niggles, limiting beliefs and clutter have been taken care of, you'll find you've created more space in your life for positive energy. What can you do to get more of this? Consider the following questions:

☆ Who and what gives you mental and emotional energy, inspiration and zest for life?

☆ What specific changes can you make to your health and well-being to increase your physical energy?

Take action to integrate these energy boosters into your day-to-day life!

Remember, to change your life you need to change your approach and motivate yourself on your own terms. What works for you as an individual may not work for someone else. The more you understand yourself, the greater the likelihood of overcoming your resistance to blocks in your life. Think back to a time when you felt motivated and in charge. What was happening around you? Connect regularly to your own source of motivation and you'll maintain the momentum to blast through any blocks!

Key Insights Gained from Step 3

☆
☆
☆

Quick Wins Gained from Step 3

☆
☆
☆

The Action Steps I Will Now Take

Action	Deadline date
☆	☆
☆	☆
☆	☆

☆ *To succeed is to accept the world as it is and rise above it.* ☆

Michael Korda

Real Results

Michael *Marketing manager, single, 30s*

Overloaded, overtired and uninspired by work, Michael was stuck in a rut, going nowhere fast. He wanted to find a new job and socialize more, but his confidence was at a low ebb, he felt too serious and didn't know how to break free.

The Value of Coaching

To help Michael spring clean his life, removing the physical and emotional obstacles in his way so he could get his energy and motivation back on track, feel less stressed and start moving on, focusing on what was really important to him.

> ☆ De-Sludge
>
> I was a bit surprised to realize this was the most impactful assignment for me. Why was I surprised? Well, it was perhaps the simplest of the activities you asked me to do. Other activities taxed my brain far more and therefore I'd have thought these would be more important. Listing the things I was putting up with helped put me in the right frame of mind to want to give coaching a go and make a success of it. I was amazed at how many things were draining my energy – piles of filing, a few broken items and bits of equipment at home, a totally overgrown garden, my car needed repairing, I was frustrated with my boss, the list went on and on. A lot of stress, which I hadn't really been aware of, was removed once I'd worked on ticking off a number of the harder items. I had more time to focus on what was important in life rather than worrying about fairly inconsequential items which I'd been putting off doing but which were very draining in terms of emotion and energy. I was then left with more thinking time and freedom. Life ceased to be a continual battle against never-ending mental lists (albeit at a very subconscious level) of things I thought I ought to be doing. It was very easy to measure

my progress. I found ticking off items was very satisfying. It was a good objective-setting exercise, both in terms of a major end result and lots of easily (sometimes!) achievable steps along the way.

✩ Limiting Beliefs

I felt totally stifled in my work, but realized I was going around repeatedly saying to myself, 'I'm not confident enough to do "x".' As soon as I noticed this, it stopped me in my tracks. When I thought about what evidence I had to prove my lack of confidence, I realized I had more reasons to show I *was* capable and confident than the other way round. I looked at my career and achievements to date and realized I was managing the largest and fastest-growing division in the group. I'd travelled a lot and led tours across Africa and always coped by myself and made the most of being in foreign parts – and my friends said they valued me for being positive, open, honest and sociable. Suddenly I realized that a more empowering belief for me would be, 'Yes, I can do that.' As soon as I acknowledged this, my life opened up. I'd just allowed my life to get cluttered and had gone into overwhelm. My 'Yes, I can do that' belief had got buried. Once I uncovered it again, I knew I could move on.

Real Results

Michael realized it was his own attitude that was the problem, not his job. He was promoted to company director and his career is now going from strength to strength, his house has become a well-organized, comfortable home, he's developed an enriching social life, feels lighter and more confident and is fitter and healthier from regular exercise and diet changes.

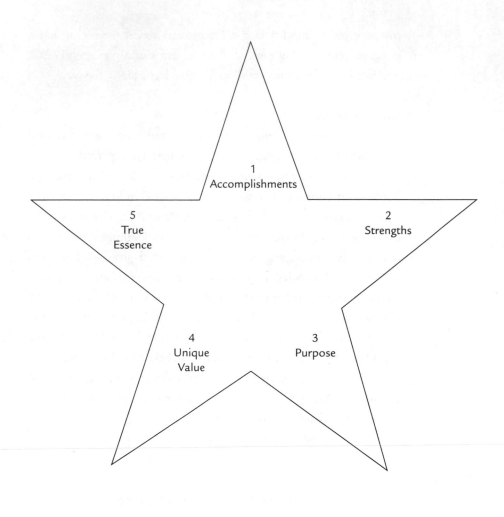

value your
true
essence

☆ *Our greatest fear is not that we are powerless. Our greatest fear is that we are powerful beyond measure.* ☆

Marianne Williamson

Overview

A key part of your life transformation is understanding and connecting with your own true self, valuing yourself for who you really are and learning to express what is special about you. I believe we are each born with a purpose and each have a unique contribution to offer the world. One of our challenges is to unlock our potential so we live our life's purpose.

How much of your day-to-day life do you spend playing to your strengths? How connected are you to your own brilliance? Are you fully aware of the impact you have on others and what they really appreciate you for? Whether in your personal or business life, the more you understand yourself and what makes you unique and the more you act upon it, the greater your likelihood of fulfilment.

Here I aim to help you to identify the seeds of your potential and to explore ways of nurturing them until they grow and come into full bloom. I want you to be happy and successful and still be true to yourself!

When you've completed this step:

> ☆ You'll be clear about your key accomplishments and the most valuable lessons you've learned in your life so far.

> ☆ You'll be integrating your strengths and abilities into your home and work life.

> ☆ You'll start to discover your purpose.

> ☆ You'll start to focus your activities around what makes you unique and where you truly add value to others.

> ☆ You'll be spending more time doing the things you enjoy and feel passionate about.

Personal Reward for Completing Step 4

☆ Write down here how you will reward yourself when you have completed Step 4:

Quick Transformation Quiz

Answer the questions below by ticking the appropriate box and calculating your score as follows:

2 points = Yes/Agree/Not Applicable, 1 point = Agree sometimes, 0 point = No/Disagree

		YES	SOMETIMES	NO
1	I am fully aware of my key accomplishments in life.	❑	❑	❑
2	I have learnt lessons from the disappointments in my life.	❑	❑	❑
3	I know what my key strengths are.	❑	❑	❑
4	I know what I'm passionate about and what inspires me.	❑	❑	❑
5	I understand the qualities that people appreciate in me and use them to help others.	❑	❑	❑
6	I am aware of the things that make me happy and spend plenty of time doing them.	❑	❑	❑
7	I am clear about the key roles that I play in my life and base my activities on the most important ones.	❑	❑	❑
8	I'm clear about what I want to be known for in life.	❑	❑	❑
9	I know my mission and purpose in life.	❑	❑	❑
10	My work is fulfilling and nourishing and I am not drained by it.	❑	❑	❑
11	I understand what's unique about me and where I add value and consistently build on these characteristics.	❑	❑	❑
12	I am very well regarded by those around me for my expertise and experience.	❑	❑	❑
13	I build on my personal strengths and delegate my weaknesses to others.	❑	❑	❑
14	I spend time doing what I love.	❑	❑	❑
15	I don't have any major hassles at work – essentially my work is more like play.	❑	❑	❑

YES SOMETIMES NO

16   I am expert at what I do and carry out my job better than most people I know.

17   I have a clear and positive career path that is moving me forwards towards greater opportunities.

18   I look forward to going to work and/or my daily life.

19   I rarely feel drained by the way I spend my day – essentially I have as much energy at the end of the day as I did at the start.

20   I feel comfortable and able to fully express myself in the work I do and in the way I spend my time.

Initial Score ☐ **Score on Completion of Step 4** ☐

Final Score on Completion of Book ☐

☆ *Love many things, for therein lies the true strength, and whosoever loves much, performs much, and can accomplish much, and what is done in love is well done.* ☆

Vincent van Gogh

Identify your Key Accomplishments and Lessons Learned

An essential part of valuing yourself and understanding your true essence is to connect with what you already know about yourself. We often forget or overlook our gifts and underestimate our achievements. I would like you to start by assessing how far you've come in your life. Write down your answers to the following questions:

☆ From a personal point of view, what are you most proud of having accomplished at this point in your life and why?

☆ How did you achieve this?

☆ What have been your biggest disappointments over recent years and why?

☆ What are the three lessons you've learned from your accomplishments and/or disappointments that you think would have the greatest impact on you if you implemented them into the next phase of your life?

 # Understand your Strengths

We all have our own special gifts and the more we use them, the more we enhance our own lives, as well as those of people around us. So often, though, we take ourselves for granted and forget what makes us special. If I were to ask you to list out your strengths and to tell me what makes you sparkle, could you answer me directly? The chances are you find it easier to list your weaknesses than your strengths. Are you hiding your light under a bushel?

As your coach I want to ensure that you connect with your true essence as much as you can in your daily life. If you're playing to your strengths and expressing your true

self, you're more likely to be enjoying yourself, feeling confident in your abilities and being appreciated by others in the process.

Your next step is to clarify what your strengths, abilities and natural gifts are. Find time over the next few days to sit quietly and complete the following exercises. You may well feel a little reluctant about doing them, but please give them a go, as when you've completed this step you'll have a much stronger sense of your own self.

Connecting with Yourself

What are you brilliant at? Where do you excel? Make a list of all your *strengths* under the following categories:

☆ Physical
☆ Intellectual
☆ Social/Relationships
☆ Business/Financial
☆ Other

Next, make a list of all your *weaknesses* in the same categories:

☆ Physical
☆ Intellectual
☆ Social/Relationships
☆ Business/Financial
☆ Other

Now make a list of the things you *enjoy* doing in the same categories:

☆ Physical
☆ Intellectual
☆ Social/Relationships

☆ Business/Financial
☆ Other

Finally make a list of the things you *don't* enjoy doing:

☆ Physical
☆ Intellectual
☆ Social/Relationships
☆ Business/Financial
☆ Other

Getting Feedback from Others

Another great way of getting in touch with your strengths and natural abilities is to ask for feedback from people who know you, whom you trust, respect and like. Sometimes other people can see our true essence more clearly than we can ourselves.

Your next task is to select five people who know you, ideally from different areas in your life, e.g. a family member, work colleague, schoolfriend or a social contact, and ask them to answer, as honestly as they can, the following set of questions about you. You may, understandably, feel a little daunted about tackling this, but I'd like you to stretch beyond your comfort zones and give it a go! Swallow your pride, take a deep breath and be willing to open yourself up to the wisdom of those closest to you. My clients often say this is one of the most useful assignments they've ever done. You can make it easier by explaining the context to people. You might want to meet up with a friend or phone them to ask them the questions and get their spontaneous replies or you could e-mail the questions and give people their own time and space to respond. Alternatively, you can make a game of it and gather together a group of friends and all share feedback on each other, so everyone benefits!

The questions to ask are:

☆ What is the first thing you think of when you think of me?

☆ What do you think is the most interesting thing about me?

☆ What do you think my greatest accomplishment is?

☆ What do you value most about me?

☆ What do you perceive to be my greatest strengths?

To obtain more lateral feedback on how others see you, a great question to ask them is: 'If I were to appear on the front cover of a magazine, what sort of publication do you think it would be and what would the article inside be about?'

Once you've received all the feedback, I'd like you to collate the information together and look at common themes.

☆ Are you starting to connect with your own source of power? Are you doing the things that make you sparkle?

☆ What lessons have you learned from these exercises? Is there a difference between how other people see you and how you see yourself?

☆ How many of the opinions you received coincide with each other? What are people's general opinions of you?

☆ Is there anything that particularly surprises you in the answers you've received?

☆ What are the key insights you've learned?

☆ What do you think your own true essence is?

☆ What three things will you do to act on what you've learned?

☆ What changes are you willing to make to play to your strengths?

☆ What will you do more of?

☆ What will you do less of?

☆ Is your life currently based around your strengths and natural abilities?

Give yourself a score out of 10 (10 being a life based totally around your strengths, 0 indicating you are not using your strengths at all):

1 2 3 4 5 6 7 8 9 10

☆ What changes are you willing to make to bring your score nearer to 10?

☆ *Try not to become a man of success but rather try to become a man of value.* ☆

Albert Einstein

Discover your Purpose

Your life undoubtedly becomes more meaningful when it is based around your purpose and core attributes. Your purpose is the essence of what you contribute to the world and to those around you, simply as an expression of who you are as a person, rather than of what you do or who and what you know. Uncovering your personal purpose can be something that comes to you quickly, in an inspired moment, or can evolve gradually during a lifelong process of discovery. A useful starting-point is to get in touch with what you really love doing.

☆ What makes you sparkle? Make a list of the three key activities in your personal life that you love doing and the three key activities in your professional life that you love doing.

☆ What comes easily and naturally to you?

☆ What is the most fulfilling, exciting part of your life?

☆ If your friends could attribute one special characteristic or quality to you, what would you want them to say?

☆ If you were going to be recognized by others as a big success at the end of the next phase of your life, what would you want to be known for?

Losing All Concept of Time in 'Flow' Activities

Another very effective way of getting in touch with your true essence is to ask yourself what you are doing when time just flies past. The chances are it's something you love. In coaching we call these 'flow' activities.

☆ List your top five 'flow' activities.

Reconnect with your Essence as a Child

It can often be useful to look back to your childhood, to a time before you were subjected to social conditioning, to gain insights into your true essence and personal purpose.

> ☆ What did you enjoy doing as a child up to the age of about seven years old? (If you don't remember, can you ask a parent or sibling or someone who knew you as a young child?)

If you can remember your core attributes as a child, these can be helpful in pointing you in the direction of your purpose. I'd especially like you to consider what qualities you had as a child. Were you independent, caring, honest, curious, adventurous?

> ☆ List your five core childhood attributes:

> ☆ What did you want to do when you grew up?

> ☆ What did your parents/guardians/friends encourage you to pursue as you grew up and how did you feel about it?

Clarify your Roles in Life

Sometimes you can start to clarify your purpose by understanding the roles you play in your life. Take a moment to list all the key roles you participate in in your day-to-day life. Are you a mother, a boss, a work colleague, a brother, a daughter, a gardener, a director, a listener, a technical person, an entrepreneur, an inspirer, a teacher, a builder? List the roles that are important to you.

Look at the roles you have written down, and in your own mind decide which are the most important for you. They could give you some inkling as to your real purpose in life.

☆ Which are the roles that are most significant in your life?

☆ Which role do you want to enhance?

☆ What is it about this role that you particularly enjoy?

☆ Where in this role do you really excel?

I would like you to make sure you're using this role to its fullest in your life.

☆ Are there ways in which you can develop or expand this role?

☆ Which roles would you like to reduce? How will you do this?

☆ What are your inklings as to your true purpose?

☆ Imagine you're already living your life as an expression of your true purpose. How would you be feeling? List three feelings.

If you can get in touch with those feelings now, in your current life, and act as if you are already living your purpose, you'll be giving yourself a head start.

> ☆ *When a woman falls in love with the magnificent possibilities within herself, the forces that would limit those possibilities hold less and less sway over her.* ☆
>
> Marianne Williamson

4 ☆ Focus on your Unique Value

We all have certain areas in our lives where we excel and it's the combination of our strengths, personal attributes and special qualities that makes each of us unique. What are your key areas of expertise? Perhaps you're superb at organizing and planning, maybe your special gift is coming up with creative ideas, managing finances or solving complex problems. The key to success is to focus on your own special qualities

☆ What are your top three unique qualities?

☆ What do you believe is the real value you bring to your personal life?

☆ What do you believe is the real value you bring to your professional life?

☆ To what degree are your current roles and your key activities focused around your unique value?

Score yourself out of 10, with 10 being totally focused on where you add value and 0 being using your abilities at all:

☆ Personal life: 1 2 3 4 5 6 7 8 9 10
☆ Professional life: 1 2 3 4 5 6 7 8 9 10

☆ What changes are you willing to make to bring your scores nearer to 10?

Once you've clarified your unique value in your personal and professional life, ask yourself what percentage of your daily life is actually spent doing the activities you're brilliant at. Ideally I want you to spend 80 per cent of your time focusing on what you do best. Is this possible for you?

☆ What changes are you willing to make to ensure you're focusing more on the areas where you genuinely add value?

Remember, focusing on where you add value will enhance your own value to those around you at home and at work and will significantly increase your personal sense of fulfilment.

5 Tap into your True Essence and Do What You Love

By acknowledging your strengths and your weaknesses you stand in your own truth. Now I want you to make the most of your strengths and to delegate your weaknesses. Can you say 'no' to tasks that don't play to your strengths? Remember, success is about knowing who you are and what you enjoy and feel passionate about and taking action and doing it! When you can tap into your creativity and use your skills and strengths in your home and work, you'll be well on your way to a fulfilling life! Give yourself the freedom to express your true self and please hold on to this thought as you work through your next transformation steps.

☆ What will you do differently now to ensure you fully value yourself?

☆ *Be faithful in small things because it is in them that your strength lies.* ☆

Mother Teresa

Key Insights Gained from Step 4

☆
☆
☆

Quick Wins Gained from Step 4

☆
☆
☆

The Action Steps I Will Now Take

Action   Deadline date

☆   ☆
☆   ☆
☆   ☆

Real Results

Alan *Entrepreneur, married father of two, 40s*

On the surface Alan was a successful entrepreneur and a happy family man who seemed to have it all. Underneath he was frustrated by the lack of balance in his life and had a deep sense that there had to be something more, but didn't know what it was or how to go about finding it.

The Value of Coaching

To help Alan get back in touch with himself, connect with his true essence and value himself more so that he could develop a strong sense of what he really wanted and a realistic plan for moving forwards.

> ☆ **Lessons Learned**
> I realized I needed a better balance between my work, family and self. I wanted a new, more lucrative work challenge to give me a greater sense of achievement and I realized I was judging my own success by how others valued me, when really I needed to value *myself* more.

> ☆ **My Strengths and Natural Gifts**
> I started by writing down my own strengths and resisted asking for feedback from other people until Carole really challenged me to give it a go. I know I'm committed to innovation, new ideas and service, but the feedback was invaluable as I'd overlooked my communication, listening and relationship-building skills and my real ability to make things happen – I just took them for granted. I realized I wasn't using these fully in my current position, which started to explain my feelings that there must be something more.

> ☆ **What I Love Doing**
> This reminded me of my love for football, which I now play most Saturdays.

☆ My Roles in Life

This helped me to clarify my ability to lead and motivate a team and led me to realize I wanted to do this, but in a new environment.

Real Results

Alan started to explore new career opportunities where he could play to his strengths. He was offered the position of managing director of a fast-growing Internet business and significantly increased his salary overnight. He's now working hard, but on his own terms, taking more holiday and spending more quality time with his wife and children, playing more football and sport in general and leading a more fulfilling life.

"The assignment that has had the biggest impact on me, I think I could describe it best as 'connecting with myself'. By really thinking about what and who I am, and what values I want to run my life by, I've gained an awareness that can often become an inner strength. Whereas in the past I've tended to chase success and happiness without knowing what it is I want, or why, I can now look at what I do in the context of a bigger picture."

☆ *Nothing splendid has ever been achieved except by those who dared believe that something inside them was superior to circumstance.* ☆

Bruce Barton

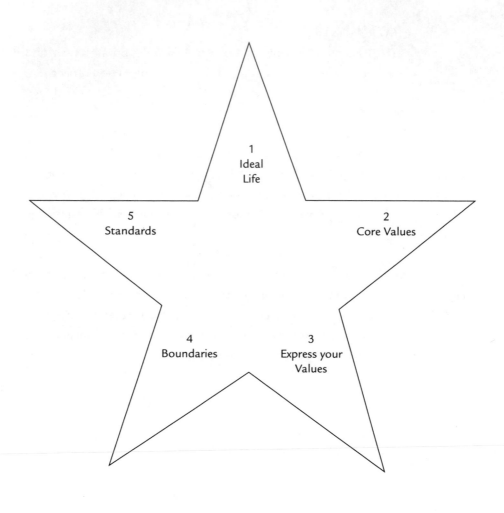

1
Ideal
Life

5
Standards

2
Core Values

4
Boundaries

3
Express your
Values

focus on what

really

matters

☆ *The great tragedy of life is
not death, but what dies inside
of us while we live.* ☆

Norman Cousins

Overview

This step is the final element of your launch pad and perhaps the most fundamental one, as it will help you to establish your values and some of the core criteria around which you can base your life decisions.

This step builds on the last one to offer you more keys to discover your true self and establish what is truly important to you. It's only when you know your values that you can start to integrate them into your life and base your decisions on them. Once you start fully expressing yourself and setting your goals based on your true values, your transformation will be more meaningful to you. I find that after completing this section my clients start to get major breakthroughs, see their lives differently and move in the direction they want to go.

When you've completed this step:

> ☆ You'll start to think about the important characteristics of your ideal life.

> ☆ You'll have clarified your own core values.

> ☆ You'll have established clear boundaries to support you.

> ☆ You'll have raised your personal standards.

> ☆ You'll have started to take action to reorient your life around your values.

Personal Reward for Completing Step 5

> ☆ Write down here how you will reward yourself when you have completed Step 5:

Quick Transformation Quiz

Answer the questions below by ticking the appropriate box and calculating your score as follows:
2 points = Yes/Agree/Not Applicable, 1 point = Agree sometimes, 0 point = No/Disagree

		YES	SOMETIMES	NO
1	I know what's important to me.	❏	❏	❏
2	I have a strong sense of my direction in life.	❏	❏	❏
3	I have clear boundaries and communicate them to those around me.	❏	❏	❏
4	I have standards and consistently adhere to them.	❏	❏	❏
5	I know what my ideal day looks like.	❏	❏	❏
6	I know what my true values are.	❏	❏	❏
7	I know what my ideal work looks like.	❏	❏	❏
8	I don't feel I have to prove myself. I accept that I am who I am.	❏	❏	❏
9	I know what my ideal lifestyle will consist of.	❏	❏	❏
10	I have a sense of inner peace and calm.	❏	❏	❏
11	I know what makes me smile.	❏	❏	❏
12	I have a deep sense of inner satisfaction and joy of life.	❏	❏	❏
13	I am well respected by the people around me.	❏	❏	❏
14	I don't allow myself to get distracted or side-tracked very often.	❏	❏	❏
15	I know what my ideal home, friends and family situation looks like.	❏	❏	❏
16	I rarely feel tied down. I feel free to do what I want to do.	❏	❏	❏
17	My life feels abundant and full of opportunities.	❏	❏	❏
18	I am not afraid or worried but instead feel confident about the future.	❏	❏	❏
19	My quality of life is on the increase. I know I have plenty of time and I have peace of mind.	❏	❏	❏
20	I am actively orientating my life around my values.	❏	❏	❏

Initial Score ❏ **Score on Completion of Step 5** ❏

Final Score on Completion of Book ❏

Imagine your Ideal Life

As you begin this section, I want you to step outside your current life for a moment and think about how you'd like your ideal life to be. This may not be an easy exercise, I know – we're all too familiar with settling for less than ideal situations. But the fundamental principle behind it is that if you're unclear about what your ideal situation would be, how can you ever move towards it?

I'd like you to spend 20 minutes on each of the following exercises. You might like to tackle them one after another or perhaps you'd prefer to address them one at a time over the period of a week or so.

Taking each assignment in turn, sit quietly, think deeply and describe your ideal scenario, listing what you perceive to be all the ideal characteristics for you for each situation. Let your imagination run riot, open yourself up to spontaneous answers, make your pictures as vivid as possible and jot down everything that comes to mind.

☆ In your ideal world, what would your perfect lifestyle, health and well-being be like? (Include your interests, hobbies, holidays, travel, training and development and details of how you would stay healthy and have fun.)

☆ In your ideal world, what would your perfect home, friends and family situation be like? (Include where you want to live and the people you want to spend your time with. How do you want to relate to others? List the key characteristics.)

☆ In your ideal world, what would be the characteristics of your perfect job or work scenario? (Include details of where you want to work and who you want to work with.)

☆ What would your ideal day look like? (What would you do and who would you be with?)

Understand your Values

Now you've started to tap into what you'd like your ideal life to look like, you'll be ready to clarify your core values. In this instance I'm not referring to your moral values, or external values, which tend to come from social conditioning or from other people, but rather those values which are very much about the essence of you as a person. They come from your innermost self and reflect what genuinely matters to you most as a person. Understanding your core values means you'll understand yourself better, feel more self-assured and be better able to make the right decisions for you. Your values will also become a strong reference point to keep your goals on track. When you focus on your values, you'll find your goals are less likely to change and you'll be less likely to get distracted by the ups and downs of life.

Before you go any further I think it's important to establish the difference between your core values and your needs, as these two elements can get confused. Values are something you find yourself naturally pulled or drawn towards. Needs are something that can drive your life, making it feel like a struggle when they are unmet. Addressing your needs is critical and we will come on to that in Step 9. For now, remember that living a life based around your core values nourishes you.

Identify your Core Values

Look through the following list of values, read each word and try to connect with the ones that appeal to you. Remember that your values are things that you're naturally drawn towards. They are very much part of your own personal make-up. An easy way to clarify your core values is to remember they are an end in themselves, not just a means to an end. For example if you select the words 'dominate field', but then realize this is only the means for you to become an expert, 'expert' is your value, not 'dominate field'. Be careful not to confuse your values with 'needs', 'shoulds' or things that actually are not 'end' values for you. Put little crosses by the words that you're drawn towards.

Values List

ADVENTURE

Risk	The Unknown	Thrill
Danger	Speculation	Dare
Gamble	Endeavour	Quest
Experiment	Exhilaration	Venture

BEAUTY

Grace	Refinement	Elegance
Attractiveness	Loveliness	Radiance
Magnificence	Gloriousness	Taste

TO CATALYSE

Impact	Move forward	Touch
Turn on	Unstick others	Coach
Spark	Encourage	Influence
Stimulate	Energize	Alter

TO CONTRIBUTE

Serve	Improve	Augment
Assist	Endow	Strengthen
Facilitate	Minister to	Grant
Provide	Foster	Assist

TO CREATE

Design	Invent	Synthesize
Imagination	Ingenuity	Originality
Conceive	Plan	Build
Perfect	Assemble	Inspire

TO DISCOVER

Learn	Detect	Perceive
Locate	Realize	Uncover
Discern	Distinguish	Observe

TO FEEL

Make	To experience	Sense
To glow	To feel good	Be with
Energy flow	In touch with	Sensations

TO LEAD

Guide	Inspire	Influence
Cause	Arouse	Enrol
Reign	Govern	Rule
Persuade	Encourage	Model

MASTERY

Expert	Dominate field	Adept
Dominate field	Superiority	Primacy
Pre-eminence	Greatest	Best
Outdo	Set standards	Excellence

PLEASURE

Have fun	Be hedonistic	Sex
Sensual	Bliss	Be amused
Be entertained	Play games	Sports

TO RELATE

Be connected	Part of community	Family
To unite	To nurture	Be linked
Be bonded	Be integrated	Be with

BE SENSITIVE

Tenderness	Touch	Perceive
Be present	Empathize	Support
Show compassion	Respond	See

BE SPIRITUAL

Be aware	Be accepting	Be awake
Relate with God	Devoting	Holy
Honouring	Be passionate	Religious

TO TEACH

Educate	Instruct	Enlighten
Inform	Prepare	Edify
Prime	Uplift	Explain

TO WIN

Prevail	Accomplish	Attain
Score	Acquire	Win over
Triumph	Predominate	Attract

Top Ten Values

Reduce your selection to a shortlist of no more than 10. Make sure that they are values and not needs. If it is something that appealed to you when you were younger, it could well be a value. If it's something that feels exciting, that you feel a little afraid of, then it's highly likely to be a value!

Top Four Values

The next stage is to reduce your values down to your top four values. Do this by grouping similar words together. Remember, this exercise is very much to do with you and how you feel about certain words, so don't allow yourself to be influenced by other people's interpretations of specific words – it's your perception that counts! Once you've grouped similar words together, choose one word from each group that sings to you more loudly than the rest. Once you've established your list of core values, choose the four that are the most important to you.

Alternative Ways to Establish your Values

If you find this process a difficult one to follow, there are several other ways in which you can connect with your values.

One way is to think back to three incidents in your life where you felt you were 'really you'. Ask yourself who you were at that time? What was important to you then? What were the common characteristics of the situation? Can you hone those characteristics down into four key words? These may well be your values.

Alternatively, think of three incidents when you were totally prevented from being your true self. What were the characteristics of these occasions? The chances are you were in a situation totally opposed to your values, so what are the direct opposites of the characteristics of the situation? Those will be your values.

☆ *I want to do it because I want to do it.* ☆

Amelia Earhart

Another useful way of connecting with your values is something referred to as the 'tombstone test'. (This is not dissimilar from some of the 'bigger picture' questions you answered in Step 1.) In this test, imagine your funeral. What four adjectives would you want people to attribute to you? Think of your close friends – how would they describe you? What about the people in your work life, what would you want them to say? It may well be that you can distil four key values from this exercise.

Express your Values

Taking each value at a time, write down your answers to the following questions:

☆ *Why this value is important to me?* List the key reasons why you selected it.

☆ *Who am I when I live this value?* Write down the adjectives that describe how you feel and act and what you think about when you embody this value.

☆ *Who am I not when I live this value?* Think about the sort of person that you are not when you have this value in your life. How do you behave and feel about life?

☆ *How well am I honouring or expressing this value in my current life?* How is this value currently impacting your life? What are you doing at the moment to express it?

☆ *Where am I not honouring or expressing this value in my life?* Where are the gaps, where is this value missing? What are you doing that is preventing you from having this value in your life?

☆ *What changes am I willing to make to express this value in my life?*
List three changes that you will make to fully express each of your values (ideas could include moving house, changing jobs, taking up a new sport, stopping smoking, sorting out your finances). When you have these three changes I would like you to transfer them to the goals pages in Step 6 (*see p.132*) for us to work on further.

Remember your values, keep them with you and when you have decisions to make in life, use your values to help you move forward in a way that is appropriate for you.

④ Establish Clear Boundaries

Once you've clarified your values and started to reorient your life around them, an important way of safeguarding this is by developing strong boundaries. Boundaries are imaginary lines that you can establish around yourself to protect you from unhealthy or damaging behaviour by other people.

Boundaries are important, because once they've been clearly communicated to others they provide a framework in which you can operate at your best. Once you have clear boundaries you can say 'no' to behaviour you find uncomfortable. Examples might be 'No, you can't put me down or criticize me' or 'It's not acceptable for you to swear in my presence' or 'Work given after 6 o'clock in the evening won't be processed until the next day' or 'We don't answer the telephone in the evening after 10 o'clock.'

Your first step is to clarify how you want people to behave around you and therefore what boundaries you want to put in place. Your next step is to explain to others what your boundaries are and how they can respect them. It is essential that you make this very clear and are consistent about maintaining your boundaries.

☆ Make a list now of the 10 things people may no longer do around you or to you.

☆ Next, identify the key people in your life you'd like to communicate your boundaries to. Sit down with each one of them, share your boundaries and get their commitment to respect each one.

If someone oversteps one of your boundaries at any time, inform them of what they are doing and request that they stop doing it immediately. If they take no heed, demand they stop. If you still don't get the response you want, walk away and make your position clear. You'll find that as you develop healthy boundaries, people around you will respect them more and they will also respect you. People who have weak boundaries are more likely to let needy and disrespectful people into their lives. Don't forget to acknowledge people who respect your own boundaries. The more you do this, the more your own boundaries will maintain themselves naturally.

Having strong boundaries also gives you the ability to grow and develop with less fear.

☆ *The secret of man's being is not only to live but to have something to live for.* ☆

Fyodor Dostoyevsky

Raise your Personal Standards

Personal standards go hand in hand with boundaries and refer to the behaviour you hold yourself to. People with low personal standards tend to have low self-esteem and may well question their own self-worth. When you develop high standards, you feel good about yourself and become an inspiration for others. Also, the higher your own standards, the more likely you are to attract high-quality people into your life.

Examples of high standards might be putting your integrity first, being honest, not gossiping about other people, being unconditionally constructive and positive whenever you open your mouth and accepting responsibility for things that happen in your life.

A useful step in helping you to raise your standards is to look back at your role models in Step 2 (*see p.62*) and identify the qualities and behaviour of these people. Think about the standards you could develop to become more like them.

> ☆ Make a list now of the 10 standards that you would like to hold yourself to in the next phase of your life (make sure you're not including any 'shoulds' or 'oughts' in your list, be true to yourself and sense which standards you're naturally ready for).

Adhering to higher standards will not only benefit you personally, but those around you as well. As you transform your life you'll have the opportunity to develop your highest self and enjoy your life more.

☆ *If you are clear about what you want,*

the world responds with clarity. ☆

Loretta Staples

Key Insights Gained from Step 5

☆
☆
☆

Quick Wins Gained from Step 5

☆
☆
☆

The Action Steps I Will Now Take

Action   Deadline date

☆   ☆
☆   ☆
☆   ☆

Real Results

Karen *Image consultant, married mother of grown-up children, 50s*

Karen wanted to make more money from her home-based image consultancy business, but was already working long hours six days a week and rarely had time for herself, her friends and family. She wanted to feel more in control of her life, manage her finances better, lose weight and feel more relaxed.

The Value of Coaching

To help Karen focus on what really mattered most to her, clarify her values, use her strengths and prioritize the important elements in her life.

> ☆ Ideal Life
>
> This exercise reminded me about my love of travel and golf, which I'd stopped having time for. I realized I wanted to become a high-profile image advisor working four or five days a week, with plenty of time to go to the gym, play sports and enjoy my family and friends.

> ☆ Clarify My Values
>
> For me the most important theme was finding out my true values. When I originally was faced with the question 'What are your values?' I must admit I was fairly clueless, never having given it any thought. The more I thought about it, the more important it became. Thinking deeply about what really mattered set the fundamental parameters in place. As I worked through the exercise, I identified my values as being 'elegance', 'energy flow', 'family' and 'accomplish'. I feel that keeping these basic values at the forefront of my life forms the guidelines by which I live my life and run my business. It doesn't mean that life suddenly becomes very easy, rather that it cuts out the extra things that don't matter.

☆ Establish Boundaries and Standards

I raised my standards by holding myself to minimum fee scales. (Before I was taking on work at little, or very low fees.) It was nerve-racking at first, but once I accepted I was worth the prices I was quoting, I started to attract clients who were willing to pay my new standard rates. I also put boundaries in place to protect my time better and told my clients the times and days I was available for consultations. I stopped seeing people on Saturday afternoons and late in the evening and my quality of life improved instantly!

Real Results

"As a result of following my values in my life I have:

☆ *Turned my workplace into a place of creativity and harmony.*
☆ *Started to play golf (about which I have become passionate!)*
☆ *Healed a year-long rift with my sister.*

I've also now joined a gym and work out several times a week, which has boosted my energy levels, and started to travel further afield on holiday (we visited Paris and the Caribbean recently)."

> ☆ *Happiness is that state of consciousness which proceeds from the achievement of one's values.* ☆
>
> Ayn Rand

real

results

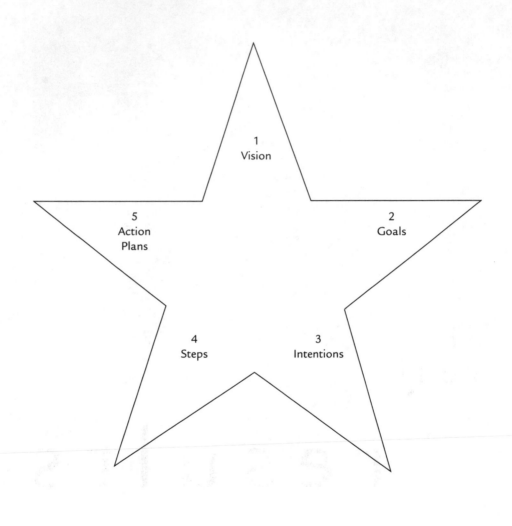

clarify your
vision
and goals

☆ *It's the set of the sail, not the blow of the gale, that determines your course in life.* ☆

Randy Davis

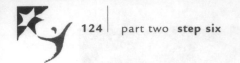

Overview

Welcome to Step 6. The fun starts here! If you've worked through the first five steps, your launch pad will be fully prepared and you'll be ready to focus on developing the big vision of the life you want to create for yourself. Congratulations!

This step pulls together everything you've been working on so far. By integrating the knowledge you've gained about who you are, your strengths, values and what matters most to you, the vision of your own transformation will become much clearer. Having a vision is an inspiring way of looking to your future. It brings you an overall sense of direction, and once you have that, it's a lot easier to set your goals and achieve your dreams!

When you've completed this step:

☆ You'll have developed an inspiring vision of your future.

☆ You'll have set genuine goals, aligned with your values and vision.

☆ You'll have clarified your intentions about what you want to create in your life.

☆ You'll have started to break your goals down into small steps.

☆ You'll be taking daily action towards moving your goals forward.

Personal Reward for Completing Step 6

☆ Write down here how you will reward yourself when you have completed Step 6:

Quick Transformation Quiz

Answer the questions below by ticking the appropriate box and calculating your score as follows:
2 points = Yes/Agree/Not Applicable, 1 point = Agree sometimes, 0 point = No/Disagree

		YES	SOMETIMES	NO
1	I have a clear vision of the life and work I want to create for myself.	❏	❏	❏
2	I am confident that I can create a compelling future for myself and those closest to me.	❏	❏	❏
3	I am excited about life and have a life plan that inspires and gives me energy to move forward.	❏	❏	❏
4	I have a personal and a career/business strategy that is working for me.	❏	❏	❏
5	I can picture the results I want to achieve in my life.	❏	❏	❏
6	I am willing and able to stretch myself and to commit to something bigger than myself.	❏	❏	❏
7	I have a strong desire to make things happen in the way I want them to.	❏	❏	❏
8	I know I am capable of achieving whatever it is I set my mind to.	❏	❏	❏
9	I acknowledge that life moves in cycles and I have a clear theme for the current cycle I am in.	❏	❏	❏
10	I spend valuable time in silence/inner reflection and/or meditation to think about my life.	❏	❏	❏
11	I am clear about my personal and professional goals.	❏	❏	❏
12	I am clear about my reasons why I want to achieve my goals.	❏	❏	❏
13	I am aware of the thoughts, beliefs or other obstacles that are blocking me from achieving my goals and am taking action to remove them.	❏	❏	❏
14	My goals do not feel like a struggle. I know they're heart felt and I am finding it easy to bring them into reality.	❏	❏	❏
15	I revisit my goals on a regular basis and am taking progressive steps towards them.	❏	❏	❏

		YES	SOMETIMES	NO
16	I know where I want to be in one year's time.	❏	❏	❏
17	I have an idea about where I want to be in five years' time.	❏	❏	❏
18	I use affirmations to support me in moving forward with my goals.	❏	❏	❏
19	Although I know the results I want to achieve, I am willing to let go and to allow things to happen.	❏	❏	❏
20	I am open and ready for the miracles to occur in my life.	❏	❏	❏

Initial Score ❏ **Score on Completion of Step 6** ❏

Final Score on Completion of Book ❏

☆ *We are what we imagine.*

Our very existence consists in

our imagination of ourselves.

The greatest tragedy that can

befall us is to go unimagined. ☆

N. Scott Momaday

Develop an Inspiring Vision of your Future

It can be difficult to see with any great certainty into the future. You may not know what your life is going to look like one year from now, let alone in three or five years' time. However, the more you think about the way you want your life to be, the more chance you have of developing a plan that is going to bring you happiness. Many business people are familiar with the concept of vision from a work perspective, but surprisingly few of us actually apply it to our own life. I want you to be clear about your vision before you go any further.

Picture your Outcome

As with anything in life, if you can start by picturing the outcome, what you want to achieve, it's much easier to make it happen. The clearer you are about what you want, the greater your likelihood of bringing it into reality.

What is the outcome you want? Starting with that and working backwards will help to keep you focused on achieving what you want.

Put Things into Perspective

Having a powerful vision helps you to put the rest of your life into perspective and will make the day-to-day pressures and small setbacks seem less important.

When your vision is really compelling, you even find yourself being pulled effortlessly towards it, rather than striving to make things happen. You can let your own vision gently pull you forward to the future of your dreams!

Develop your Three-Year Vision

I would like you to start by focusing specifically on the next three years. Imagine you're revisiting this book three years from now. Allow yourself to look back over the last three years of your life to the present day.

☆ What would have to have happened over the past three years, both in my personal and work life, for me to feel happy and pleased with my progress?

Develop your One-Year Vision

I'd now like you to develop a one-year vision for your life. A detailed one-year focus is usually best for most people, although it can be helpful to see it in the context of a three- or five-year time-span.

Give yourself 20 minutes or so to jot down your thoughts about how you want your life to be a year from now. Write it down in the present tense and be specific. What do your personal life, your work, your home and family, your health and well-being, your finances, your relationships, any other important elements look like to you? How do you feel? Who are you as a person? Describe as best as you can what will have to happen for you to be happy in the knowledge that you've achieved your desired results.

My Vision for my Life in One Year's Time

Describe the following in as much detail as you can:

☆ Personal life, home and family
☆ Work/business life
☆ Health and well-being
☆ Finances
☆ Relationships and community
☆ Intellectual and/or spiritual life
☆ Other

Create a Destiny Map

You may find that a useful way of clarifying your vision is to create a destiny map. A destiny map is a visual representation of what you would like in your life. It can help you to make your dreams tangible by using pictures and symbols to create reality. A useful timeframe to use in a destiny map is between one and three years.

To create your own destiny map, get yourself a large poster board. You'll need a wide variety of magazines, pictures, crayons, glue, scissors and anything else you think might be useful in starting to create pictorially the life you want to live.

Simply go through the magazines and cut out any images or symbols that represent the things you would like in your life – a house in the country, a specific type of car, a family you would like to have, pictures of the sort of work you would like to be doing or hobbies you would like to pursue. Stick the pictures on the board and create a collage of your new life.

How much money would you like to be earning? Some people find that by pinning either Monopoly money or bank notes on the board or even writing themselves out a cheque for the amount of money they would like to be earning focuses their mind on what it is they'd like to create.

Build your picture as fully and as colourfully as you can. Don't make the board too cluttered, keep it clear and focused on the key elements – unless you want your life to be cluttered!

This can be a really fun exercise to do and the more focused your attention and the more energy you put into it, the more powerful your destiny map will be. You may find you want to have a go with friends, and let them create their maps while you're creating yours. Some people like to create a destiny map as part of their meditation process, when they sit quietly and let the thoughts come to them and then find the images and the pictures to create their own boards.

Once you've completed the destiny map, put it in a place where you can look at it regularly. Let it become a constant reminder of how you want your life to be. A good idea is to look at it just before you go to bed and then allow your subconscious mind to work on it while you sleep.

☆ *The game of life is a game of boomerangs. Our thoughts, deeds and words return to us sooner or later, with astounding accuracy.* ☆

Florence Scovel Shinn

 ## Set Genuine Goals

Now you have your vision and values, you are ready to set your goals for this phase of your life transformation. Your goals will set you in motion. As soon as you start acting on your goals, you'll be surprised how much your energy increases.

Revisit the Goals You've Set So Far

Let's go back and pick up the original goals you wrote down in Step 1 (*see p.44*). Revisit the three specific goals you set yourself for the year ahead and the three goals you set for the next three months. Are these in line with your one-year vision? Have you made any progress with them to date?

Quickly review the work you carried out on your strengths, essence and purpose in Step 4 (*see p.91–101*). Have these insights sparked any further thoughts on your goals? Also take a look back at Step 5 and refresh your memory about the changes you agreed to make in your life for your four core values to be fully expressed (*see p.114*).

My Top 10 Goals for the Next Phase of my Life

I'd like you to combine all the insights gained so far with your one-year vision and focus on setting your top 10 goals for the next phase of your life. When you set the right goals for yourself, you will feel excited, a little nervous, ready and willing to *go for it!*

Make your Goals SMART

SMART means making your goals Specific, Measurable, Attainable and Realistic within a given Timeframe.

Be specific and detailed about what you want and where possible quantify each goal, so you can easily measure your progress. Be realistic and set goals that are within reach (even if that requires effort on your part). If you set your goals too high, you may become discouraged; conversely, if you set them too low, they won't stretch you enough. I don't want you to lose motivation or the momentum needed to make them happen.

Proceed at your own pace, but make sure you do take action. By setting a deadline, you can have the courage to be exact. If you want to double your income by a specific period or stop smoking for Christmas or get out of debt by the end of the year, make this clear. Remember, a goal without a deadline is just a pipe dream. Discipline yourself and set a date.

☆ *The man who has no imagination has no wings.* ☆

Muhammad Ali

Ensure your Goals Are Genuine

The following is a quick checklist to ensure you've clarified the right goals. Ask your-self the questions below to check that your goals are in alignment with who you are and what you really want:

☆ *Does this goal keep me moving towards who I want to be?*
Ensure that your goals are in harmony with the overall theme of your life and don't detract from it.

☆ *Are my goals in alignment with my values?*
Make sure you're not working towards a goal that conflicts with your values. If your goals are consistent with your own inner beliefs, your ability to achieve them will never be undermined.

☆ *Do my goals truly come from my heart and not just my head?*
Ensure that each goal is something you genuinely want rather than something someone else thinks you should have. If the goal is right for you you'll find synchronicity starts to step in. (We'll talk about this more in Step 10.)

The Specific Measurable Goal	Start Date	Finish Date
1		
2		
3		
4		
5		
6		
7		
8		
9		
10		

3 Clarify your Intentions

It's all well and good writing down a clear set of goals but if you really want to create a lasting life transformation you need to have lots of reasons to support *why* each goal is important to you – you need to develop clear intentions.

You can't underestimate the power of intention. It's your intention to do something that will really bring about conscious change. The energy from your intention itself has the power to organize events and make it happen. As Deepak Chopra says in his *Seven Spiritual Laws of Success*, 'Through your intent, you can literally command the Laws of Nature to fulfil your dreams and desires.'

For each goal, ask yourself, 'If I attain this, what will it give me?' Take some time to write down the *big benefit* of achieving each goal. If ever you falter when working towards a goal, reminding yourself of the big benefit will help to keep you motivated.

☆ What is the *big benefit* of accomplishing each goal?

When you've written your list, put it in your diary or journal or post it on the fridge or the mirror in your bathroom, wherever you're going to look at it regularly.

Identify the Pain associated with Not Achieving Each Goal

Connecting strongly with the benefits of achieving a certain goal is a powerful way to keep yourself motivated. However sometimes reminding yourself of the pain you're likely to feel by *not* accomplishing the goal could be an even stronger incentive. Remember, the more you get in touch with what it's costing you to stay where you are, the easier you'll find it to overcome any obstacles in your way.

☆ Look back at your goals list and write down the pain associated in not accomplishing each of your goals.

What Personal Strengths Can Help You Bring Each Goal into Reality?

As you connect with each goal, remind yourself of your strengths and consider which you can make use of to help you reach each goal more easily.

What Specific Challenge or Potential Block Could Prevent You from Achieving Each Goal?

☆ What is in the way or could stop you from achieving each goal?

☆ What will you do to overcome the obstacle or block? Do you need to develop any new skills or get someone to help you?

4 Break your Goals Down into Small Steps

The goals you've selected may be large or small. The chances are, if you're serious about transforming your life, some of your goals are likely to be big ones. Good for you – congratulations on setting yourself a challenge!

I don't want you feel overwhelmed by any of your goals – remember, you can eat the elephant one bite at a time! Breaking your goals down into manageable chunks helps you to devise sensible action plans for them. Setting intermediate targets helps you make a start and build momentum. If you want to achieve a certain weight loss in a specific period of time, for example, you might want to break that goal down into weekly and monthly goals.

The motivational expert Napoleon Hill said, 'Conceive, believe, achieve.' If you believe you can achieve something, you will. Simply take your first steps towards it and as you become more confident, the subsequent steps become easier.

Develop a Three-Step Action Plan for each Goal

☆ List below the first three action steps you're willing and ready to take to move each of your key goals forward:

Goal 1 ☆
☆
☆

Goal 2 ☆
☆
☆

Goal 3 ☆
☆
☆

Goal 4 ☆
☆
☆

Goal 5 ☆
☆
☆

Goal 6 ☆
☆
☆

Goal 7 ☆
☆
☆

Goal 8 ☆
☆
☆

Goal 9 ☆
☆
☆

Goal 10 ☆
☆
☆

Integrate Action Plans into your Daily Life

Goals are worthless unless they're followed by action. I want you to focus on making each one of your goals happen. The more you work on your goals on a daily basis, the more you're likely to achieve them. Think about ways you can incorporate elements from each of your goals into your daily routine, so they become a natural part of your life. List them in your daily inspiration journal, read them every morning and evening and remember that as you repeat them in your subconscious mind, they'll become embedded and more real.

Pay Regular Attention to your Goals

Paying regular attention to your goals will help speed up the transformational process. Look at your destiny map regularly and remind yourself of the big benefits of your goals every now and again. Remember, if you keep your goals realistic and SMART, 'what the mind can conceive, it can achieve'. Any goal that truly fires your imagination and fills your heart with joy is reachable. (Make sure you focus your attention on what you want in your life, and not on what you don't want, as putting your attention on the negative might bring it into being!)

Develop Affirmations

Why not use affirmations to support you in moving your goals forward? Affirmations expand your beliefs and stimulate your imagination.

A great way of developing affirmations is to give yourself a series of positive present tense statements describing the benefits of your goal and how you'll feel when you reach it. Your statements can be short, but make them believable yet exciting. Either write them down or read them out or even record them onto a cassette for playing in your car or at home. If you say them aloud at bedtime, they're likely to enter your subconscious mind, which will assimilate them as reality while you sleep.

Act as if your Goal is Already in Existence

From the moment you're clear about your goals, I want you to start acting as if they are already in existence. If you act in a successful way from the very beginning you're much more likely to achieve the results you want. Don't wait for things to happen to you – the more you act as if they're here now, the sooner they'll come to you.

Key Insights Gained from Step 6

☆
☆
☆

Quick Wins Gained from Step 6

☆
☆
☆

The Action Steps I Will Now Take

Action	Deadline date
☆	☆
☆	☆
☆	☆

Real Results

Andy *Finance director, married, 40s*

Andy was at a crossroads in his life. He had already reached a peak in his career and had recently left his job wanting to do something different, but he didn't know what. His personal life felt stale and unfulfilled. He and his wife wanted a family, but he was always so busy and it was never quite the right time.

The Value of Coaching

To help Andy develop a clear sense of direction and purpose and a realistic personal and professional life plan so he felt in control of his life and was spending more time doing the things he wanted to do.

Real Results

"I decided to reject a full-time job and pursue a 'portfolio' career as an independent director working for several different businesses in part-time roles. I had concerns about this initially — that it would be less interesting, a backward step in my career and that it might not work at all, leaving me with a cash-flow crisis! The lifecoaching process helped me to overcome these concerns and gave me the courage to give it a go.

I now have three immensely fulfilling roles helping young companies with their strategies to expand, raise capital and achieve their ambitious goals. Better still, there seems to be no short-age of opportunities and hopefully I will soon have a full portfolio of five or six companies. Apart from the independence, this gives me variety, a sense of making a real contribution and importantly, more time to pursue other goals in life.

Through the True Values programme, I discovered a hidden aspect of my character, which so far had been totally unfulfilled — the need for creativity. Since my coaching, I have taken on some ambitious house and garden design projects at home, designed and built my own website and taken up creative writing. My wife and I are now working together on a business project based at home, which is both fun and fulfilling. Most importantly of all, we are expecting our first baby.

One final change I have made as a direct result of lifecoaching is to live more for the moment. I had always felt I was working towards some long-term goal or paradise, but Carole helped me to see that the important time is now. So I try and do things I will enjoy today, rather than things that might lead to greater happiness down the line. All in all, I'm very happy and enjoying life to the full again, a far cry from my aimless wanderings last summer! Both my wife and I seem to be putting more in to life and getting more out of it, which is how it should be, I guess. We're even getting up earlier – a worrying trend!"

Angela *Network marketer, married mother of one, 30s*

Angela had a big dream – to create a healthier, more balanced life for herself and those around her. She wanted to build her network marketing business to a point where it was financially stable enough for her husband to leave his job and join her in the business, so they could work together and spend more time at home with their young son.

The Value of Coaching

To help Angela clarify her vision and develop realistic goals, so she could start living her dream.

☆ **Destiny Map**

This really helped to bring my vision alive, I created my board using pictures to depict my ideal home and work life and the money I wanted to be earning. I keep it in my office at home and look at it daily to remind me of what I know I can achieve – it keeps me inspired when I have to make those phone calls!

☆ **My Intentions**

I want to help people create more balance in their lives and am determined to build a business that helps people do that. I see the benefits of what I'm doing every day with feedback from customers and colleagues, plus I get to see my husband and son much more than many people see their families, so I know I'm on the right track!

☆ Affirmations

I recorded my own affirmations tape that I listen to every day in the car as I drive my son to and from school. It has helped me build my confidence and move forward with small steps each day.

Real Results

Angela has now successfully integrated her business and family life. She has set up a new office to work from home and organized systems to make her more productive. Her business is growing steadily, so much so that she qualified for a free holiday in the US. Angela has now increased her income enough to enable her husband to leave his job and join her in their business. With more time to spend with her son and on playing badminton and keeping fit, Angela is well on her way to developing a fulfilling life.

☆ *People begin to become successful the minute they decide to be.* ☆

Harvey Mackay

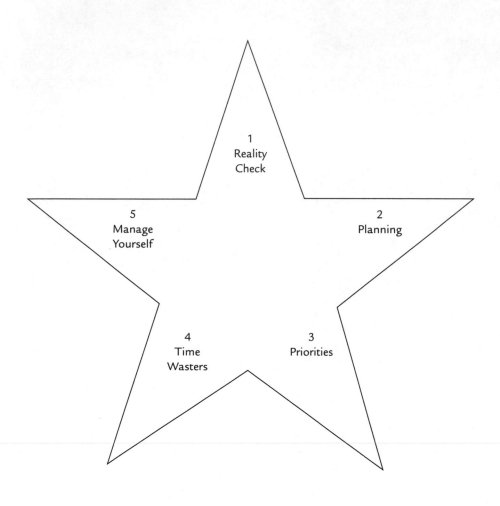

1
Reality
Check

5
Manage
Yourself

2
Planning

4
Time
Wasters

3
Priorities

make time
work
for you

☆ *Nothing is impossible to a willing heart.* ☆

John Heywood

Overview

Time is one of the most valuable gifts you can give anyone – including yourself! We're all so busy these days that the ability to make the best use of time is an important factor in determining our happiness and success.

You may be working towards your vision and goals, but unless you're managing your time effectively, you'll find yourself disappointed with your progress. It goes without saying that the more you get time on your side, the more satisfaction and less stress you will have in your life!

In effect, managing time is more to do with how we manage ourselves than anything else. We can't control time but we can control ourselves. The more effective use you make of your time, the quicker you'll see your life transform!

When you've completed this step:

> ☆ You'll have taken a reality check, monitored how you currently use your time and started to make improvements.

> ☆ You'll be taking the time to plan and will have set up an effective time management and planning system for yourself.

> ☆ You'll be focusing on your important priorities and will be investing your time wisely.

> ☆ You'll have eliminated the time wasters from your life.

> ☆ You'll be managing time on your terms, building reserves, monitoring and evaluating your performance and consistently achieving more in less time.

Quick Transformation Quiz

Answer the questions below by ticking the appropriate box and calculating your score as follows:

2 points = Yes/Agree/Not Applicable, 1 point = Agree sometimes, 0 point = No/Disagree

		YES	SOMETIMES	NO
1	I am self-disciplined and perfectly able to manage myself.	❏	❏	❏
2	I am persistent and willing to take determined action towards achieving my goals.	❏	❏	❏
3	I have plenty of time to do the things I want to do.	❏	❏	❏
4	My personal life and work life are well integrated and in balance.	❏	❏	❏
5	I am realistic about how I spend my time and about the length of time it takes to accomplish specific tasks.	❏	❏	❏
6	I identify my key priorities on an ongoing basis.	❏	❏	❏
7	At any one moment I am clear about what is the single most important investment in my time.	❏	❏	❏
8	I am quite ruthless in assessing my priorities and maintain them as a focal point in my activities.	❏	❏	❏
9	I make time daily to plan.	❏	❏	❏
10	I have a clear framework for making the most effective use of my time and I stick to it as long as it serves me wisely.	❏	❏	❏
11	I commit to deadlines and consistently deliver on time.	❏	❏	❏
12	I regularly under-promise and over-deliver.	❏	❏	❏
13	I rarely procrastinate but maintain myself in the flow.	❏	❏	❏
14	There are no blocks to my productivity.	❏	❏	❏
15	I have plenty of time for developing new projects or pursuing new opportunities.	❏	❏	❏
16	I am always on time and ready for meetings and do not rush.	❏	❏	❏
17	I am willing to say 'no' and am clear when to do a task myself or delegate it.	❏	❏	❏
18	I finish things properly so they don't come back to annoy me.	❏	❏	❏
19	I am continually innovating and improving the way I work and the things I do.	❏	❏	❏

	YES	SOMETIMES	NO
20 I have the right systems and all the equipment I need to support me and enable me to be fully productive.	☐	☐	☐

Initial Score ☐   **Score on Completion of Step 7** ☐

Final Score on Completion of Book ☐

Take a Reality Check

How do you spend your time? Have you ever stopped to think about how productive you are and whether you're getting the most out of the time you have? As you begin this step I want you to answer a few questions about your current time management.

☆ Rate yourself on a scale of 1 to 10 as to how well you think you are managing time (1 being badly, 10 being perfectly):
1 2 3 4 5 6 7 8 9 10

☆ What activities took up the largest proportion of your time last year?

☆ What was the most valuable use of your time last year?

☆ What were your three biggest time wasters last year?

☆ How many days' holiday did you take over the last year?

☆ Approximately how many days (and hours per day) did you spend working?

Start a Seven-Day Time Tracker

For many of us achieving more in less time is a highly desirable goal that can seem difficult to realize. It is impossible to find more of something you don't actually know you've lost, so the greater your awareness of how you spend your time, the easier you'll find it to take action to improve it. The perfect starting-point is to establish your current reality by tracking your use of time over a seven-day period.

> ☆ If you had to categorize the seven key activities you spend your time doing during an average week, what would they be?

Keep a track of how you spend your time, minute by minute, hour by hour, day by day, for the next seven days. The easiest way of doing this is to use your journal or keep a diary close by your side. Log in, as honestly as you can, everything you do with your time. Create a time tracker using the seven key categories you identified earlier and add an eighth heading: 'Miscellaneous Activities' (these can include a whole variety of things that occur less frequently). Simply record how much time you spend doing each of the activities. Make sure you log interruptions and time-wasting activities. Don't leave it to the end of the day to record your details – where possible carry your time tracker with you and make notes as you go, as the chances are your delayed information will not be as accurate as your spontaneous recordings.

> ☆ *Keep true, never be ashamed of doing right. Decide on what you think is right, and stick to it.* ☆
>
> George Eliot

For example, if you are a business person you may want to record how much time you spend working on the computer, doing your administration or working on new business development or client relationships. If you are a mother based at home your time tracker may well include time spent preparing meals, collecting the children from school, shopping and household chores.

You might find the prospect of undertaking this exercise a little daunting, but I can assure you that the end results will more than outweigh the effort! It may be difficult to start with, but you'll find you improve with practice.

Once you've tracked your time for seven days I would like you to summarize your key findings, being as honest with yourself as possible. Work out percentages for each category.

☆ What percentage of your time did you spend doing which activities?

☆ How do your time tracker findings compare with how you *want* to be spending your time?

☆ What were the greatest surprises to you in your tracking study and what were the key lessons you learned from the exercise?

☆ *Enthusiasm finds the opportunities, and energy makes the most of them.* ☆

Henry Hoskins

Take the Time to Plan

Now you've established how you *are* spending your time, the next step is to clarify how you *want* to spend your time. We all have 8,760 hours in our year, but it's our choice what we do with them. I encourage you to set up a clearly planned time management system tailor-made to your own needs and key activities.

The more you organize your time, the easier you'll find it to create space for spontaneity. It might seem somewhat of a paradox, but those who fail to plan and structure their time often find themselves more restricted, with less free time, than their well organized counterparts!

If you're someone who resists using a time planner, the chances are you're likely to benefit from it most! Once you get into the habit of planning ahead, your life will flow more easily. I want you to set time aside regularly to plan your future and monitor your progress towards your goals. Use your diary or planner and block out specific personal and business planning time as follows:

Yearly Overview

Schedule in one day's 'personal think-tank time' every year to give you your annual focus for what you want to achieve in the coming year. This is often great to do at New Year or around your birthday, when you're likely to be more inclined to focus on your goals for the year ahead.

Also plan in your key tasks, holidays and special events, family occasions and regular meetings, so you can start to see how you want your year to look and the key results you want to achieve at specific times.

An Overview Every Three Months

It is useful to monitor your progress and track your goals every three months, so plan in three hours at a time to do this.

Monthly Overview

Plan in an hour once every month to review your key activities for the month ahead, clarify important events and highlight the particular results you want to achieve during the coming month.

Weekly Overview

Set aside time at the end of each week to plan the week ahead, check meetings and important arrangements and determine the best use of your time for each particular week. Setting yourself three key goals to achieve each week is a great way of keeping yourself focused on your priorities.

Daily Review

Finally, allow 15 minutes at either the start or the end of each day to set your schedule for the day ahead, so you create a daily plan before you do anything else. Ask yourself, 'What is most important about today?' and make sure you prioritize this above everything else.

☆ *Identify your problems,*

but give your power and energy

to solutions. ☆

Anthony Robbins

Plan your Time in Blocks

Categorize your key activities and block out specific days or times in the week to do them. Planning your day in blocks and allocating specific lengths of time to certain activities will help to keep you focused and on track. Be realistic about how long things take and when your time is up on one activity, make sure you discipline yourself to move on to the next task. This way you will make measurable progress on each task and not let yourself get bogged down! If you're a visual person you might like to use a highlighter pen and colour in allocated blocks of time on your planner.

Build in Time for the Unexpected

It's a fact of life that you'll get interruptions in your day-to-day life that you can't foresee. To some degree they may be out of your control. Allowing for contingency time is vital in helping you to keep control of your life. I want you to create space for the unexpected, so make sure that you allocate time in your daily schedule to handle interruptions and unscheduled events. Also, give yourself a few hours 'catch up' time every once in a while to deal with any backlog of tasks that may have built up. Provided you give yourself this extra buffer within your schedule, the chances are that you'll have the flexibility to handle more or less anything that's thrown at you!

Create Time to Withdraw and Recharge

Don't forget to block out time for yourself, where you simply relax and recharge your batteries. However busy you are, when you take regular time to withdraw and recharge you'll find it's easier to maintain high levels of efficiency, productivity and an inner sense of calm. Taking five-minute breaks regularly throughout the day, having a lunch break or time out sitting quietly, taking a walk, breathing deeply and feeling peaceful will increase your levels of concentration and your ability to achieve more in less time.

Identify your Priorities

I'm sure that most of us will acknowledge that the more we focus on the priorities in our life, the more quickly we are likely to achieve our desired outcomes. If you've already spring cleaned your life, removed many of the distracting obstacles in your way and become clearer about your own strengths and values, you'll be ready to focus now on what's important. Remember, highly successful people are very focused – they recognize their priorities and strengths and delegate the rest. Focusing on priorities also helps you to avoid getting side-tracked by those unimportant yet urgent activities that can take over your day-to-day life, as no doubt you discovered in the time-tracking exercise! Make your time work for you by concentrating on the most important priorities, so you can achieve a lot more in less time.

Investing your Time Wisely: The 80/20 Rule

We all have the same 24 hours in a day but sometimes it doesn't feel like enough time. It's a fact of life that there is often more for you to do than you can possibly do in the time available. So you need to make wise choices about how you invest your time and energy. It's as important that you're doing the right things as much as you're doing things right!

I'd like you to think for a moment about the 80/20 rule. That is, 20 per cent of all your activities are likely to produce 80 per cent of the meaningful results in your life. Think for a minute. What is your 20 per cent? What is the small handful of activities that will really produce the key results in your life?

> ☆ What are the three things that will make the biggest difference to your life and work and move you towards your vision?

Once you've completed this exercise I'd like you to really think about the top 20 per cent as being your 'gold time' activities. The more time you spend working on these activities, the more quickly you'll see your life transforming. Make sure you make inroads into these tasks with every opportunity you get. At every odd moment try to keep doing things that move your gold activities along. Remember, don't procrastinate, do these activities now, don't waste time on non-focused activities.

Remember to make sure that your gold focused time is spent doing what you genuinely do best. If you're unsure about this, go back to Step 4 and reconnect with your strengths and your own value. Remember, the more you spend your time playing to your strengths, the more fulfilling it will be.

Focus on a Maximum of Three Priorities

I want you to ensure you focus on no more than three important activities so you give them as much time as you can. This is often a huge challenge to many of my clients. It's very tempting to take on more. But if you're serious about making a success of your life, maintaining your focus is imperative. It requires self-discipline and the ability to say 'no'. Too many of us spend our time rushing around, chasing our tails, coping, solving problems and fire fighting. This is not what I want for you. When you lose sight of your key priorities, it's impossible for you to be effective.

> ☆ *To love is to give one's time. We never give the impression that we care when we are in a hurry.* ☆
>
> Paul Tournier

Integrate your focused priorities into your yearly planner. Review your goals from Step 6, align them with your gold time activities and then list your top three priorities for the following time periods:

My Top Three Priorities for the Year Ahead

☆

☆

☆

My Top Three Priorities for the Next Three Months

☆

☆

☆

My Top Three Priorities for the Next Month

☆

☆

☆

As you fill in these sections, think about your answer to the questions:

☆ If nothing else gets done this year, what would I be happy with achieving?

☆ If nothing else gets done in the next three months except x, what would that be?

And so on. Obviously you'll be reviewing your general priorities on a weekly and daily basis, but the importance of clarifying your priorities, tracking and monitoring them cannot be overemphasized.

☆ *If it doesn't absorb you,*

if it isn't any fun, don't do it. ☆

D. H. Lawrence

4 Eliminate Time Wasters

If you've been truly honest with yourself during the time-tracking and priority exercises, I'm sure by now you'll have started to be a great deal clearer about the drains on your own time and the changes you want to put it into place to make the best use of your time.

As your coach I want you to stop doing anything that is a waste of your time. That might sound like quite a harsh statement to make, but it's critical if you really want to transform your life and achieve more in less time.

We all get distracted and interrupted from time to time. You'll know what the time wasters are for you – and I want you to keep them to a minimum. Unexpected visitors, crisis management, telephone interruptions, a cluttered home, office or desk, personal disorganization, unclear objectives, the lack of a daily prioritized plan, unnecessary meetings or a lack of your own self-discipline are key culprits. I want you to cut them out of your life now.

Taking on Too Much

Trying to do everything yourself can be a huge time waster. Taking on the whole world may feel heroic, but is highly unlikely to be in your best interests. Become a master of delegation! You've already done plenty of work on clarifying your strengths and priorities. Focus on these and delegate as much of the rest as you can.

Part of managing your time effectively is not only knowing what to concentrate on, but also what *not* to do. It's a human tendency to lull ourselves into a false sense of security thinking that we are the only people who can do a specific job. It's easy to become reluctant to delegate any tasks to an assistant or to outsource it to some-one else completely. Accept that even if the task isn't exactly up to your standards, as long as it's done well enough, let it be. Remember, you need to play to your strengths. If you're someone who has trouble handing work over to others, realize the benefits of paying someone else to do what you don't enjoy or what you're not good at. Whether that's paying someone to clean your house or taking on an extra member of staff to handle some of the routine tasks at work, do it!

> ☆ Make a list of the top 10 tasks that you can delegate,
> to whom you'll delegate them and when.

The Power of 'No'

We touched upon the power of 'no' in Step 3, but it's worth mentioning again here. Saying 'no' is a skill that takes practice to do pleasantly. I trust that by now you're becoming a master at it, so you have more space to focus on what's important to you. A straightforward 'no' is best, but you might want to soften it in your own way.

As already mentioned, you may find it useful to buy yourself time before responding to a request immediately. 'Can I get back to you?' can be a very valuable question. Just allowing yourself a few seconds, minutes or hours could give you the opportunity to suggest a better solution that doesn't involve you!

> ☆ Are there any more things in your life that you need to say 'no' to?

Perfectionism

Another major culprit of time wasting is having an attitude of perfectionism. If this is holding you back, try and focus on making progress and taking steps towards the end result rather than making things *perfect*. You'll find the more you focus on the results you want to achieve, the less important the actual activities to get you there become.

> ☆ What are you trying to make perfect in your life and what are you
> willing to do to free up your time and energy around this?

Procrastination

Procrastination is the art of putting things off and many of us are extremely skilled at it! Are you someone who can be very creative in thinking up excuses? Putting things off and/or leaving them to the last minute can mean you waste a considerable amount of time and effort worrying about them, causing yourself stress and undermining your ability to take charge of your life. The only way to break out of this is to just get on and take action.

A great way of blasting through procrastination is to identify the most unpleasant job on your 'to do' list, and tackle it first, before you do anything else. Psychologically this will set you up for success – everything else will seem easy, once you've tackled the worst task! Alternatively, break a large onerous task down into small chunks and allocate, say, 15 minutes every day to chipping away at it steadily so you feel as though you're making progress effortlessly!

☆ What are you procrastinating about? List everything, select the worst item on your list and just do it!

☆ What three things can you stop doing this week that will stop you wasting your time?

☆ *People who have no time don't think. The more you think, the more time you have.* ☆

Henry Ford

Manage Time on your Terms

Create Healthy Time Habits

It's not uncommon to feel overwhelmed by the sheer magnitude of what needs to be done to transform your life. But as you create healthy, regular habits to manage your time, you'll find your levels of self-confidence rising. As well as creating healthy habits, educate other people about your habits – they will gradually get used to them! Consistency is the key here. When you want to make a change, do it and stick with it. Routines make things a lot less painful. If you can implement a few routines and be clear about what they are, you'll find your life runs a lot more smoothly.

One of the most useful habits you can develop is to regularly ask yourself: 'Is this the best use of my time?' This will keep you on track and ensure you're not wasting any precious time. Once you've set up a system of making time work for you, keep a close eye on what's working and what isn't and make changes where necessary.

Build Reserves

Are you constantly dashing around trying to adhere to unrealistic deadlines? There's nothing worse than putting yourself under pressure, letting the adrenalin pump through your body when you make promises you know you're going to struggle to meet. Remember to build in a time buffer – having reserves of time enables you to operate at your best, with less stress. If you arrive at appointments 5 or 10 minutes ahead of schedule, for example, you have time to get your thoughts together and make the most of the meeting.

As well as time reserves, build up physical reserves of commodities you use often. Not only does this save you the time and hassle of regular shopping trips, but also physical stocks of things are a constant reminder to you that you have established substantial reserves in your life and have more than enough to help your life flow easily. (Examples of this might be holding stocks of stationery, toilet paper, wine, or anything else that supports your lifestyle.)

Another secret of managing your time is to manage other people's expectations and 'under-promise and over-deliver'. By this I mean promising someone less than you know you can deliver. This relieves the pressure on you and helps you to optimize your time. When a person expects less and then receives more, they see you as very efficient and you become very attractive to them.

☆ What can you do to build in reserves of time in your life?

Honour your Personal Energy Cycles

Are you a morning or an evening person? When is the best time of day for you to do specific activities? Are you best handling phone calls first thing in the morning or is the morning your best time for being quiet, writing and thinking, planning and developing? When is the best time of the day for you to be outgoing? When is it best for you to focus on concentrated activities?

Our personal energy cycles vary. If you become aware of yours, you can plan your days, weeks and months accordingly. You may well find your energy levels vary on different days in the week. Monday might be a good day for you to do administrative tasks and to be internally focused whereas a Friday might be a day for you to be out and about. Think about where different tasks can best be fitted into your day and build these in as part of your routine.

We all have our own rhythm and sense of pace. Relax and become aware of yours and of those around you. Use the insights to plan accordingly.

☆ What changes will you make to honour your own personal time and energy flows?

☆ What is the best use of your time right now?

Key Insights Gained from Step 7

☆
☆
☆

Quick Wins Gained from Step 7

☆
☆
☆

The Action Steps I Will Now Take

Action	Deadline date
☆	☆
☆	☆
☆	☆

Real Results

Rachel *Business owner, divorced, mother of two, 30s*

With the pressing needs of a growing business and a young family to deal with, Rachel felt she was running around in circles with never enough time to focus on anything properly. She wanted to be a good mother and a successful business person, but she felt constantly stressed with no time for herself, let alone time to go out and meet a new partner.

The Value of Coaching

To help Rachel balance her home and work life and manage herself superbly so she could plan ahead, focus on her priorities, delegate effectively and make the best possible use of her time.

☆ **Reality Check**

This brought me down to Earth with a bump. I realized I was trying to be all things to all people both at home and at work. My health was starting to suffer and I knew I needed to do something about it. I was wasting time at work doing lots of small but necessary administrative jobs and never sat down at home as I was always doing things for the boys, plus household chores and many endless tasks. Carole challenged me to delegate anything that wasn't the best use of my time. I reassessed my childcare arrangements and wrote a detailed job description and task list for the nanny. At work I employed an office manager to take over the day-to-day responsibilities of managing the office and restructured my team and their responsibilities, so I could focus on what I do best, which is developing new business and working with key clients on important projects.

☆ **My Priorities**

The boys came first and building my business was second. However I realized if I didn't prioritize my own well-being, we would all suffer.

I started to block out time for myself, joined a gym, visited a nutritionist and a complementary practitioner and made my health a key priority.

☆ **Building Reserves**

In a fairly simple way the concept of building reserves really helped me. My life tends to be very busy and I realized that through building reserves I could reduce the stress and make it more manageable and enjoyable. This can be through fairly simple things from ensuring my car never runs out of petrol to always having some money in my wallet. It also means building energy reserves by looking after myself by taking exercise and eating well. These all seem fairly basic but it is amazing how they add up and can cause so much hassle. Life seems so much more manageable if I can just manage my reserves.

Real Results

Rachel become more proactive in managing her business and her life. She moved the business forward and tripled the turnover. Restructuring her staff, clarifying their roles and delegating tasks freed her up to concentrate on her important priorities. As she rearranged her childcare and became fitter and healthier due to a better diet and regular exercise routine, she started to have more time, space and energy for her social life. She has now found a new partner to share her life with.

☆ *There are only two ways to live your life. One is as though nothing is a miracle. The other is as though everything is a miracle.* ☆

Albert Einstein

☆ *Destiny is not a matter of chance, it is a matter of choice. It is not a thing to be waited for, it is a thing to be achieved.* ☆

Jeremy Kitson

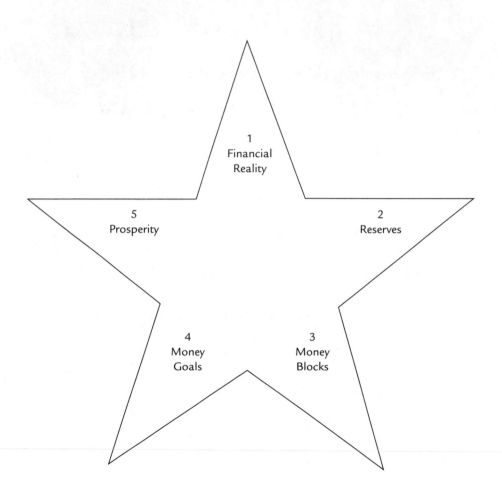

shape up

your

finances

☆ *Wealth is the product of man's*

capacity to think. ☆

Ayn Rand

Overview

A fundamental part of transforming your life is establishing a firm financial platform from which to operate. When your financial situation is in order it's much easier to be yourself – you tend to feel a lot healthier, you can lead a relatively stress-free life, are more relaxed and able to focus on your key life goals. In essence, money provides you with the means and the energy to create your dreams.

As your coach, I want you to shape up your finances so they work for you, give you energy and support you. I want you to feel totally in control of your money and of your financial reserves and have a savings plan that makes you feel responsible not just for now, but for the future as well. Your finances are often a litmus test of your level of self-worth and also give an indication of your willingness to invest in yourself as a person. If you want to live a fulfilling life, taking charge of your finances is a crucial element.

Many people tend to have a love-hate relationship with finances. If you're a person who enjoys the financial side of life, the chances are this step will be a relatively easy one for you to take. However, if you're someone who tends to bury your head in the sand when financial issues arise, I suggest you work your way steadily through this step. Be patient with yourself. Just by making a start you'll soon begin to gain financial confidence and make progress.

When you've completed this step:

☆ You'll fully understand your current financial situation.

☆ You'll have taken charge of your finances by reducing debt and expenditure, building up your savings and setting up a financial support system.

☆ You'll have acknowledged your beliefs and blocks about money and the impact they have on your life.

☆ You'll have clarified your financial goals.

☆ You'll be taking action towards opening yourself up to prosperity.

Personal Reward for Completing Step 8

☆ Write down here how you will reward yourself when you have completed Step 8:

Quick Transformation Quiz

Answer the questions below by ticking the appropriate box and calculating your score as follows:
2 points = Yes/Agree/Not Applicable, 1 point = Agree sometimes, 0 point = No/Disagree

		YES	SOMETIMES	NO
1	I am totally honest with myself about my money situation.	❏	❏	❏
2	I know what my expenditure levels are and live on a weekly budget which allows me to save.	❏	❏	❏
3	I live well within my means and always pay my bills on time.	❏	❏	❏
4	I have repaid any borrowings or have a clear plan as to how I will repay any monies owing to others.	❏	❏	❏
5	My source of income or revenue is predictable and relatively stable.	❏	❏	❏
6	I have savings that I can fall back on as and when I need to.	❏	❏	❏
7	I am currently saving a minimum of 10 per cent of my income.	❏	❏	❏
8	I understand my own beliefs about money and if any one of them is holding me back I am taking action to address it.	❏	❏	❏
9	I am protecting myself and am well insured, both with personal insurance and insurance policies for my key assets.	❏	❏	❏
10	I am fully up to date with my taxes and do not have any legal issues hanging over me.	❏	❏	❏

		YES	SOMETIMES	NO
11	I have made a will and update it regularly where appropriate.	❏	❏	❏
12	I know I am earning what I deserve.	❏	❏	❏
13	I don't worry about my finances or investments.	❏	❏	❏
14	I have a clear financial plan for the year ahead.	❏	❏	❏
15	I have a vision for my financial future. I am clear about how to become financially secure and am on track.	❏	❏	❏
16	I am saving money on a regular basis to enable me to reach a state of financial independence.	❏	❏	❏
17	I have multiple income schemes to support me and am generating passive income for my future.	❏	❏	❏
18	I never feel held back by money or the lack of it.	❏	❏	❏
19	I have people around me who will support me with my financial plans.	❏	❏	❏
20	I feel relaxed about money and am ready and willing to open myself up to abundance.	❏	❏	❏

Initial Score ❏ Score on Completion of Step 8 ❏

Final Score on Completion of Book ❏

☆ *The strongest single factor in prosperity consciousness is self-esteem: believing you can do it, believing you deserve it, believing you will get it.* ☆

Jerry Gillies

Establish your Financial Reality

Tell the Truth about your Finances

How honest are you with yourself about your financial situation? Are you totally clear about how much you spend, how much you earn, how much you save? Do you have a strategy in place to make yourself financially secure and independent?

☆ Are you in full control of your finances? How would you rate yourself on a score of 1 to 10 (1 being no financial control, 10 being total control over your financial situation)?
1 2 3 4 5 6 7 8 9 10

☆ Do you have a positive attitude to money? Rate yourself from 1 to 10 (1 being negative beliefs about money such as 'I don't like to think about or discuss it', 10 being a very positive attitude towards money such as 'I enjoy and look after it'):
1 2 3 4 5 6 7 8 9 10

☆ Do you expect to have as much money as you need? Rate yourself from 1 to 10 (1 being 'Money is scarce, there's never enough', 10 being 'I expect money to flow to me, there's always more than enough'):
1 2 3 4 5 6 7 8 9 10

☆ Do you live within or beyond your means?

☆ Are you a natural saver or a regular spender?

Perhaps unsurprisingly, many of us dread knowing the truth about our financial situation. It's not uncommon to be vague about your expenses, about how much you spend and where your money goes at the end of the week or at the end of the month. In general we all spend at least 10 per cent more than we realize. Strengthening your financial situation is not necessarily as difficult as it may seem. In essence when you get yourself to the point where you have no debt and you're consistently saving around 25 per cent of your income you're on track to financial independence. It can be as easy as that!

Establish How Much You're Worth

A key starting-point in clarifying your financial reality is to establish how much you're currently worth. Make a start by valuing your assets and liabilities. Don't be put off by this – we can make it fairly straightforward. You simply need to look at the Net Worth table below and fill in the relevant values. Add up the value of everything you currently own (this can include property, cars and any other valuable items), add insurance policies, savings and investments and money in the bank and deduct from this the value of any debts – mortgages, loans, the outstanding amounts on credit cards and bills. To help you, you'll find values on your annual statements. If you don't have these you can telephone the customer help desk of your provider and ask for a statement to be sent to you. All financial service providers will be very happy to do this and it is a very common request. If you have any miscellaneous items, add them to the relevant columns at the end.

☆ *Abundance is not something we acquire. It is something we tune into.* ☆

Wayne Dyer

Assets and Liabilities	£ Now	£ Future
ASSETS:		
House/property		
Car/vehicle		
Investment properties		
Endowments and insurance policies		
ISA/PEP/TESSA		
Building society accounts		
Equities or shares		
Investment club		
Unit trust or investment trust holdings		
Pensions		
Antiques		
Jewellery		
Cash in the bank		
Spare cash		
Other valuables and assets		
Subtotal: All assets		
LIABILITIES:		
House mortgage(s)		
Business loans		
Private loans		
Loans from work, friends and family		
Credit card debt		
Account card debt (e.g shop cards)		
Hire purchase		
Overdue bills		
Other loans and debts		
Subtotal: Liabilities		
Total: Net worth		

To arrive at your total net worth, add up all your assets and total all your debts or liabilities, then deduct the value of your liabilities from the value of your assets.

☆ My actual net worth is £ ......

☆ What would you like your net worth to be? £ ......

☆ Are you worth as much as you want to be? Rate yourself out of 10, with 1 being nowhere near where you want to be and 10 exactly where you want to be: **1 2 3 4 5 6 7 8 9 10**

Clarify your Current Income and Expenditure

If your net worth is lower than you want it to be, being honest about your real income and expenditure levels is fundamental to taking charge of your finances.

Take a look at your income pattern over the past year and work out what your average monthly income is. Does your income vary from month to month or is it relatively stable?

☆ My current average monthly income is £ ......

If you're not fully aware of the true extent of your monthly outgoings, take time to work them out. You may find it useful to track your actual expenditure over the next month and keep a detailed list of everything you spend. Keep a track of your big monthly bills as well as your tiny daily purchases. Summarize them at the end of the month and see how much you really spend.

☆ My current average monthly expenditure is £ ......

Take Charge of your Finances and Build Up Reserves

Having acknowledged the reality of your financial situation, I now want you to take full charge of shaping up your finances. Money worries are a huge energy drain. It's virtually impossible to transform your life if you're being dragged down by financial insecurity and a negative cash flow. The sooner you can address these issues, the better!

Get Out of Debt

The initial stage of the money merry-go-round is to get out of debt. If you have debts – credit card debts, loans, overdrafts and borrowings – take full responsibility for them and work at erasing them from your life.

You might want to consolidate your debts, cut up your credit cards and check you're paying the lowest interest rates on outstanding loans.

Some people find a great way of managing their expenditure is to cut up all their credit, debit and store cards and simply operate with cash. If you think this could work for you, why not spend the next three months operating on a cash-only basis. This will help you to keep track of exactly where you are and how much you're spending. If you draw a set amount of cash at the beginning of every week, your challenge is to live off that without extending yourself.

Reduce your Expenditure and Plug Money Drains

Having taken a look at your income and expenditure patterns and clarified where your money goes, I want you to look at ways in which you can reduce your monthly expenditure by between 10 and 30 per cent. It's not how much you earn that determines your financial situation, but how much you keep!

How can you trim back your expenditure? You might like to enlist the help of a friend to go through your expense records and see where you can cut back. If you both do the exercise at the same time, you can challenge each other to cut down. Why not have a reciprocal arrangement in which you help your friend to reduce their outgoings by 25 per cent and they help you to do yours?

☆ List at least five things that you can start doing to reduce your expenditure.

Many of us spend money on things that really we don't need. Think about money spent on sweets, magazines or any items that you really never use. Also consider whether you're paying too much for your insurance or the mortgage on your home. Maybe you could reduce the amount of tax you pay.

☆ I challenge you to find 10 ways in which you spend your money that actually isn't rewarding to you.

Create a spending plan for yourself. Make it realistic. Record how much you actually spend against how much you plan to spend and look at the difference. Don't spend more than you make. Work with your plan for six months and then take a rain check and decide how you're progressing.

Start Saving for the Future

Financially successful people tend to save at least 20 per cent of their income. What are your savings plans? Have you looked at your pension recently? What does your investment portfolio look like?

Embarking on a major savings initiative might be too radical for you at the moment, but do *something* now, even if the step you take is a small one. If you begin saving an extra £5 per week and work up to 10 per cent of your income, this is a step towards success. Take it – you'll be glad you did.

☆ What actions will you take to start saving?

You might need to use your own creativity for this and also brainstorm ideas with a friend, but if you simplify your lifestyle and also start to save, what you're doing is giving yourself freedom for the future. You're starting out on a track towards financial security and independence. Whether you save an additional £10, £100 or £200 a week, it is all an investment towards your future. Maintaining one month's living expenses in your current account and three months' expenses in a savings account will provide you with a good financial platform.

Set up a Financial Support System

As you start to cut down your expenditure, reduce your debts and develop savings plans, you may well find that you need to work with a friend who is good with money or a financial adviser.

To really set yourself up for financial success you may want to consider investing in a financial software package for your computer or changing your bank, employing a book keeper, an accountant or a financial planner. If this is necessary, the first thing is to find someone who you can trust.

Understand What Holds You Back Financially

Before you move on to setting your financial goals for the future, it's important to take a look at anything that might hold you back financially. You may have developed unhealthy money habits, think your finances are unimportant, hold limiting beliefs about your ability to earn money or not trust yourself to effectively manage your finances. Unless you address these issues, you'll find it very difficult to create future financial security.

☆ What mistakes do you repeatedly seem to make with money?

☆ What lessons have you learned in the past from your finances?

Clarify your Beliefs about Money

Understanding the beliefs you associate with money is crucial in finding your own path to financial security. Your attitudes are very likely to influence what you think is possible. What you believe is the reality you project into the world. I want you to understand your defining beliefs about money and decide which ones are useful to you and which ones are no longer appropriate in your life.

What are your fundamental beliefs about money? Do you believe there's always enough to go round? Do you think you have to work hard to earn your money? Do you ever say, 'I'm not worth it', 'I'm broke', 'I'll survive', 'I'll scrape by' or 'Money doesn't grow on trees'? Are you afraid that people might not like you if you become too successful financially? Do you make regular comments to yourself and those around you about money? Disempowering self-talk about money issues is some-times referred to as 'negative money scripts'. What are yours? I'd like you to listen to yourself over the next week and become aware of any complaints or phrases you use with regard to money.

> ☆ List your negative beliefs and any disempowering things you say
> to yourself about money.

If you've been holding negative beliefs about money it won't be easy to change them overnight. But if you sincerely want to open yourself up to financial prosperity, then it is possible, step by step, to change your negative beliefs to more empowering ones. (Revisit Step 3, *p.80*, for more insights.)

I would like you to look at each belief in turn and think about how you can turn it into a more empowering one. Can you turn your negative belief on its head and come up with a statement that is really going to serve you in a positive way? Look for evidence and role models around you to support your new empowering belief. When you take your mind to the negative money script you hold, acknowledge the judgements you make about money and say silently to yourself, 'I reject these beliefs. They're not for my highest good or for the highest good of anyone else involved with me. I want to change and replace this script with a positive one which serves my highest good.'

Let go of any resentment. Alongside every negative belief you've listed, add the new empowering belief that you agree to work on in the next phase of your life. Examples of empowering beliefs include:

☆ 'I deserve to make money or own "x".'

☆ 'I can make/earn more than enough without struggling.'

☆ 'Money is recognition for my experience, time, effort, so it's OK to make money.'

Address Emotional Blocks

Your relationship with money can tell you a lot about yourself. For example, if your money is out of control the chances are some part of your emotional life is also out of control. If you're stingy and tight with money it may well be that you're afraid of love and intimacy. If you're worried constantly about running out of money, perhaps you're afraid of being left alone. If you never have enough money, ask yourself whether it is because you believe that you are not worth enough. If you often say, 'I'm broke', do you actually feel broken or wounded inside for some reason?

If you're always borrowing money from other people, ask yourself whether you think you deserve more than you receive emotionally and whether you can get those emotional needs met elsewhere. If you find money slipping through your fingers and never feel as though you can have enough for yourself, is this perhaps because you don't think you deserve prosperity? If you need to be rescued financially, this may be an indication that you may be feeling needy, alone or unloved.

As your coach I want you to be very honest with yourself. If there's something that's holding you back on an emotional level it may well be that your money situation is a physical manifestation of it. At the end of the day, money is a reflection of the universal flow of energy in your life. If there are blocks at some level, the more you work to remove them, the more easily your life will flow.

☆ Do you have an emotional block about money that you think could be holding you back?

☆ What you can do to tackle this? Who can help you?

☆ What new financial truths would you like to create for yourself about money?

 # Set your Financial Goals

Now you've got to grips with your current financial situation, I want you to start focusing on your financial future. You've probably already set yourself some specific financial goals in Step 6. Now I want you to think about your future and what financial security means to you. Money is essentially a means to an end – it funds a lifestyle. What do you want money for? What will a specific level of income or financial security give you? Do your best to answer the following questions as fully as possible:

☆ What would it take for you to feel financially secure?

☆ What would you like to earn, save and invest to know you are financially independent?

☆ What is currently blocking you from achieving financial independence?

☆ How does your current financial situation impact on your goals and plans for your life transformation?

☆ In what way is your current financial situation holding you back from living the life you want to live?

Open Yourself Up to Prosperity

As you work on your plans for generating your own financial security I want you to remain open to the possibility of creating whatever money you need in your life. The more you're able to open yourself up to the possibility of abundance, the greater the likelihood of you experiencing abundance in your life! I want you to be open to receive the ebb and flow of money. See it as an energy exchange, as a process of give and take. Money goes out and money comes in. Recognize wealth in your life and acknowledge your own true wealth. When you feel worth the money you want to have, you'll find yourself attracting it more easily and will be in a strong position to make your financial goals a reality.

☆ How much of a priority is making more money for you?

Acknowledge Abundance

Many people build their lives on the principle of scarcity or lack, believing there is never enough to go round. This becomes a self-fulfilling prophecy as they go about their day-to-day life struggling to make ends meet. Abundance and scarcity are both a matter of perception. Once you change your perception, feeling and action will follow.

I want you to come from a place of abundance. The starting-point for this is to appreciate how much abundance you already have in your life. In the Western world we live in a land of plenty – our homes are full of luxuries, clothes, furniture and equipment we rarely use, we are surrounded by friends and most of us enjoy lives of relative prosperity. Do you suffer from poverty consciousness? Do you hear yourself saying 'I can't afford that' or 'It's too expensive'? Beliefs of scarcity and lack are caused by social conditioning. I want you to let go of anything or anyone who is undermining your own sense of self-worth.

> ☆ What are the areas of lack or scarcity in your life? What are you
> willing to do about them?

Let go of any habits of poverty. Give your loose change to people in need and open yourself up to the possibility of receiving positive energy in return.

Abundance is very much a state of being and a measure of the confidence you have about life. I want you to cultivate feelings of confidence and richness in your life on an ongoing basis. Recall a time in your past when you felt a deep sense of richness, remember how you felt and hold onto these feelings now. I want you to give off an air of abundance, then others will reflect this back to you.

If you cultivate a rich sense of being, act as if you're already living in abundance, this will help to create the momentum to bring more abundance into your life. Don't forget, whatever you perceive, you receive.

A useful way to bring abundance into your life is to develop appropriate affirmations that you know you believe in deep down. 'I live in a world of abundance' repeated regularly every day may start to move you onto new levels of financial well-being.

> ☆ What changes can you make to open yourself up to abundance?

> ☆ What do you need to do to feel worth more in yourself?

> ☆ Are you ready to move to the next level financially?

As your coach I want to help you move towards financial freedom, so you regularly gain enough income to more than meet your own needs. If you want to increase your income, why not think about your top 10 ways of earning more money? Do you need to update and refine your business or career plan? Do you need to do more training or learn new skills? In your current job, is it appropriate for you to ask for a pay rise? Move jobs if you need to and start to develop a plan to attract a higher-paying job before you leave.

Here are a few more thought-provoking questions:

    ☆ What actions could you possibly take to double your
       current salary?

    ☆ List all the things that you could do to bring in extra cash.

Sometimes people find that securing themselves an extra job in addition to their main job helps their cash flow in the short term. (If you're contemplating this, however, please think carefully about the implications extra work could have on the rest of your life. I want you to maintain a healthy work/life balance, so don't over-commit yourself!)

Income can come from multiple sources. To improve your financial situation, start diversifying your activities towards those that give you the highest return. Make sure you associate with role models who are earning money and are a good influence on you financially. There are plenty of ways of creatively generating extra income. Why not get together with a group of friends and see what ideas you can come up with?

    ☆ Make a list of things you could do to improve your financial
       situation, things which you would respect and admire yourself for.

Start doing them!

Key Insights Gained from Step 8

☆
☆
☆

Quick Wins Gained from Step 8

☆
☆
☆

The Action Steps I Will Now Take

Action   Deadline date

☆   ☆
☆   ☆
☆   ☆

Real Results

Sally *Manager, single, 30s*

Sally was tired and run down and feeling increasingly negative and disillusioned with her job and where she lived. Her finances, confidence and energy levels were at a low ebb. She wanted to get her enthusiasm back and have some more fun in her life.

The Value of Coaching

To help Sally take responsibility for her life, develop a positive attitude, address her sense of self-worth, shape up her finances and move her life onto the next level.

☆ **Reduce Money Drains**

I cut down my expenditure by changing the mortgage on my house and paying off my credit card debts. I rather reluctantly took up the challenge to lock away all my credit and debit cards and live off cash for three months. It was really hard at first, but after a week I realized how many things I had stopped myself from buying because I didn't have sufficient cash on me. It gave me a shock, but I felt stronger and more responsible, which funnily enough, increased my self-confidence! I stopped spending money on useless bits and pieces like make up, impulse clothing purchases and magazines. I even cut back enough to start investing more in my pension and started saving £50 per month in a high-interest savings account. I immediately started to feel in control of my life and much better about myself.

☆ **Beliefs about Money**

I realized I'd conditioned myself to thinking, 'I'll scrape by.' This helped explain why I was not achieving what I wanted to financially. As soon as I had the awareness about how I was sabotaging myself, I started to do something about it. Instead of believing I could scrape by, I rewrote the script to say: 'I have more than enough.' Carole encouraged me to build reserves of things to remind me of the abundance in my life. Coaching gave me the confidence to believe in myself and reinforced my sense of self. Building up reserves in both material and non-material things – buying mundane items in large quantities so that you don't have to think about them very often – helped me value myself more. I hadn't extended this to money reserves and coaching helped me see the value of that.

☆ Set Financial Goals

Once I'd got a handle on my own worth and was feeling more positive about what I had to contribute, I was able to set a specific target for what I wanted to earn. It was a bit of a challenge, but I wanted to stretch myself. Two months later I was offered a job with a package that actually exceeded my target!

Real Results

Sally got a new job and the increased salary and benefits she wanted. She cut down her commuting and has the possibility of working from home on occasions. Now, with a stronger financial base and more time, she has joined a gym, started going to salsa and dancing classes and got her life back.

☆ *The biggest human temptation is*
to settle for too little. ☆

Thomas Merton

☆ *Men often become what they believe themselves to be. If I believe I cannot do something, it makes me incapable of doing it. But when I believe I can, then I acquire the ability to do it even if I didn't have it in the beginning.* ☆

Mahatma Gandhi

☆ *You can get everything you want if you help enough others get what they want.* ☆

Zig Ziglar

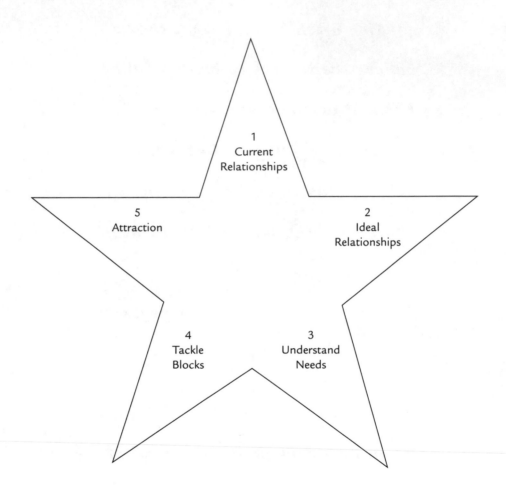

attract the
relationships
you want

☆ *The deepest need of man, then, is*

the need to overcome his separateness,

to leave the frisson of his aloneness. ☆

Erich Fromm

Overview

The quality of your relationships, both with yourself and with other people, will have a significant impact on your overall sense of fulfilment. The more attractive you are to yourself, the more attractive you will be to others, and the easier and more enjoyable your own life transformation will become. At the end of your life it's unlikely you'll be thinking about how hard you've worked or how much money you've earned. True happiness is not based on your possessions, your power or your image, but on the quality of your relationships with people you love and respect.

I want you to create fulfilling one-to-one connections and a vibrant network of great relationships that will nurture you as you design the next phase of your life. I want you to surround yourself with people who can expand your horizons and help you to be more of who you are.

You might be able to achieve an incredible amount by yourself, but when you're connecting with the right people, you'll be amazed how your life can be propelled forwards! With this in mind, I want you to become connected to like-minded individuals and people who inspire you.

As technology continues to transform the planet and the way we live our lives, the world is becoming smaller. Your relationships and communities need no longer be restricted to local people. You might want to consider building a global network for yourself or becoming a member of a world-wide group.

When you accept yourself and allow your true essence to shine brightly, you'll be in a strong position to develop empowering relationships with others. I want you to have a strong sense of yourself, so you sparkle with real confidence and attract 'quality' people to you on your own terms.

When you've completed this step:

☆ **You'll have established the reality about the relationships in your life now.**

☆ You'll be clear about the relationships you want and the characteristics of the people you'd like to attract.

☆ You'll have improved the relationship you have with yourself, started to open your heart, understand your own needs and get them met.

☆ You'll be tackling any outstanding negative relationship issues and blocks, so you can gain a deeper connection with yourself and others.

☆ You'll have learned how to improve your communication and relating skills so you can attract more enriching, synergistic relationships into your life.

Personal Reward for Completing Step 9

☆ Write down here how you will reward yourself when you have completed Step 9:

☆ *Love has nothing to do with what you are expecting to get, only with what you are expected to give... Which is everything.* ☆

Katherine Hepburn

Establish the Reality of your Relationships

Your Relationships with Others

I believe nobody is in your life by accident, without a specific purpose or reason. Think about the people you're surrounding yourself with now. How are they reflecting where you are in your life and what are they teaching you?

☆ How do you rate the quality of the current relationships in your life on a scale from 1 to 10 (1 being very poor relationships, 10 being the best relationships you could ever wish for)?
1 2 3 4 5 6 7 8 9 10

☆ Who are the most important people in your personal life?

☆ Write down next to each of the people on your list what you particularly value about them and what you're learning from them.

☆ Who are the most important people in your business/ professional life?

☆ Again, write down what you particularly value about each person and what you're learning from them.

☆ Select your top three to five relationships. Are you spending as much quality time as you want to with the most important people in your life? How much time would be enough with each person and what changes are you willing to make to improve things?

☆ What can you do to stay connected and maintain communication with the other key people in your life?

☆ Who have been the five most influential people in your past?

☆ What have been the key lessons these people have taught you about yourself?

☆ What would you do differently now as a result of lessons learned from your past (and present) relationships?

☆ How do you think the people around you would currently rate your communication skills? On a scale of 1 to 10 (1 low, 10 high) rank how the following people would rate your communication skills:

  ☆ close family member
  ☆ your best friend
  ☆ business associate
  ☆ team member

Your Relationship with Yourself

If you want to build significant relationships in your life, whether with a loved one, friends, family, a client or colleague, it's important to address and strengthen your relationship with yourself first. The more you believe in yourself and respect yourself, the more others will believe in and respect you. The more attractive you feel on the inside, the more this will be reflected on the outside and in the world around you.

In Steps 4 and 5 you have gained more understanding about your strengths, your unique qualities and your values. Have you started to integrate these qualities into your everyday life? Are you expressing yourself fully as the person you know you are? Self-belief and self-confidence are very attractive qualities to possess. Also, confidence is catching. The more confidence you have in yourself (or appear to have), the more others feel confident in you. Equally, the more you believe in yourself, the more others will believe in you.

Respect for yourself is key to acknowledging your talents and abilities and under-standing what you can give to others. When you recognize your own self-worth you'll also be better able to respect others for who they really are. It is by respect-ing others that you attract good things to yourself.

☆ How do you rate your relationship with yourself?
Rank yourself from 1 to 10 (1 being disconnected
from your true self and dissatisfied with who you are,
10 being totally happy and relaxed with yourself):
1 2 3 4 5 6 7 8 9 10

☆ How do you rate your self-worth?
Again, rank yourself from 1 to 10 (1 being little
self-worth, 10 being you know you deserve the best,
you fully value and believe in who you are and how
you are contributing to the world):
1 2 3 4 5 6 7 8 9 10

☆ How confident are you?
(1 not at all confident, 10 totally confident)
1 2 3 4 5 6 7 8 9 10

☆ Do you think you're capable of attracting and
maintaining high-quality relationships in your life?
(1 no, 10 definitely) **1 2 3 4 5 6 7 8 9 10**

☆ What changes would you be willing to make to move your
scores closer to 10?

Clarify the Relationships You Want in your Life

Now you've established where you are with the relationships in your life, I would like you to clarify who you want to share the next phase of your life with. Which people do you want to include in your life? What personal qualities are you looking-ing for and what kind of interactions do you want to have?

Unless you have a clear vision of the type of relationships you want in your life, it's going to be very difficult for you to actually make them happen. Before you tackle the following assignments, you might want to revisit the visioning exercises in Step 6 (*see pp.127–8*).

☆ Who do you want to attract into your personal life? List the types of relationships, roles and interactions you're looking for (whether that's a significant other or relationships with friends and family).

☆ From a business/career point of view, what relationships and interactions would you like?

☆ Take each of the relationships you've listed in turn and think about what would be ideal about it for you. What are the most important characteristics and qualities of each relationship for you?

☆ Of the relationships and qualities you've listed, which ones do you already have in your life now?

☆ What relationships or qualities and characteristics are currently missing in your life?

I think it's important to point out here that whilst I've asked you to think about what your ideal relationships would look like, you will not necessarily find *all* your ideal qualities in one person. No one and nothing is perfect all of the time. If you can attract relationships that are 80 per cent of your ideal, you'll be well on your way to creating a happy and fulfilling life for yourself. If you can accept – or perhaps even enjoy – some imperfections in a relationship, your life will be enriched in the process.

Identify Synergistic Relationships

As you identify your ideal relationships, I'd like you to think how you can benefit from the power of synergy in your life. Synergy is where the whole is greater than the sum of its parts. 1 + 1 does not equal 2, but 3 or maybe even more. Synergy holds true in relationships where the interaction between people sparks off far greater possibilities than the sum of the achievements of the individuals by themselves. It is very much aligned with the idea of teamwork. The more you value the differences between yourself and others and let those differences blossom into something greater than each individual could manage alone, you are opening yourself up to the power of synergy.

Be aware of the people around you with whom you could have a synergistic relationship. Keep yourself open to possibilities. Inspiration and support can come from unexpected areas. These might include people or groups who see things differently from you but whose opinions you respect. I want you to connect with people who will open your mind and offer you opportunities that could create something bigger for you as a person.

☆ List the people, networks, communities and groups who
you think will help you to grow during the next phase of your life.

Once you've clarified who these people are, make plans to establish regular contact with them so you build strong relationships to move yourself forward.

Connect with Yourself and Understand your Needs

An essential part of attracting quality relationships into your life is making sure you understand your own personal needs and discover healthy ways to get them met so you're approaching your relationships as a 'complete', 'unneedy' person. We all have needs, but if you're not careful, trying to get them met within the confines of a key relationship can spell disaster.

We all need air, food, water, shelter, light and love in order to live. There are also our own personal needs, which we often allow to go unnoticed. Personal needs are the qualities we must have in our lives in order to be ourselves. They often tend to be the things we've not been able to get enough of in our lives for some reason.

Until you understand what your own personal needs are and how they can be met, they'll have a tendency to drive you or make you feel incomplete in some way. If you don't address them, they can gradually build up and prevent you from fully engaging in high-quality relationships.

The very first stage in handling your needs is to be willing to acknowledge that they exist in the first place! Once you recognize a need and start to take action towards satisfying it, the less of a hold it has on your life.

It can take time to get your needs met and everyone's time-scale varies. Be aware of this and honour your own personal timing process.

Identify your Personal Needs

Begin by reading through the following list, which describes the more common needs, and identify your top 10 needs. I find the easiest way of doing this is to read through the words first and put a cross by any that brings out a very strong reaction in you, either positive or negative. You might find that some of the words make you blush or even shake. These could be signs that they are needs for you. Be willing to look at words that you would normally pass over. These may be hidden needs which could be extremely important to you.

If you find it difficult to clarify your key needs, don't worry, this process can be a gradual one. A useful question to help you really understand your needs is: 'What will that give me?'

It may well be that you have a hierarchy of needs. You may start with one word and ask what that will give you, but the answer to that question may well take you to another word, which is perhaps a deeper need. Again ask yourself: 'What will that give me?' This may well lead you to a third answer, which is your core need.

ACCEPTED

Approved	Be included	Respected
Permitted	Be popular	Sanctioned
Cool	Allowed	Tolerated

TO ACCOMPLISH

Achieve	Fulfil	Realize
Reach	Profit	Attain
Yield	Consummate	Victory

BE ACKNOWLEDGED

Be worthy	Be praised	Honoured
Flattered	Complimented	Be prized
Appreciated	Valued	Thanked

BE LOVED

Liked	Cherished	Esteemed
Held fondly	Be desired	Be preferred
Be relished	Be adored	Be touched

BE RIGHT

Correct	Not mistaken	Honest
Morally right	Be deferred to	Be confirmed
Be advocated	Be encouraged	Understood

BE CARED FOR

Get attention	Be helped	Cared about
Be saved	Be attended to	Be treasured
Tenderness	Get gifts	Embraced

CERTAINTY

Clarity	Accuracy	Assurance
Obviousness	Guarantees	Promises
Commitments	Exactness	Precision

BE COMFORTABLE

Luxury	Opulence	Excess
Prosperity	Indulgence	Abundance
Not work	Taken care of	Served

TO COMMUNICATE

Be heard	Gossip	Tell stories
Make a point	Share	Talk
Be listened to	Comment	Informed

TO CONTROL

Dominate	Command	Restrain
Manage	Correct others	Be obeyed
Not ignored	Keep status quo	Restrict

BE NEEDED

Improve others	Be a critical link	Be useful
Be craved	Please others	Affect others
Need to give	Be important	Be material

DUTY

Obligated	Do the right thing	Follow
Obey	Have a task	Satisfy others
Prove self	Be devoted	Have a cause

BE FREE

Unrestricted	Privileged	Immune
Independent	Autonomous	Sovereign
Not obligated	Self-reliant	Liberated

HONESTY

Forthrightness	Uprightness	No lying
Sincerity	Loyalty	Frankness
No withholds	No perpetrations	Tell all

ORDER

Perfection	Symmetry	Consistent
Sequential	Checklists	Unvarying
Right-ness	Literal-ness	Regulated

PEACE

Quietness	Calmness	Unity
Reconciliation	Stillness	Balance
Agreements	Respite	Steadiness

POWER

Authority	Capacity	Results
Omnipotence	Strength	Might
Stamina	Prerogative	Influence

RECOGNITION

Be noticed	Be remembered	Be known for
Regarded well	Get credit	Acclaim
Heeded	Seen	Celebrated

SAFETY

Security	Protected	Stable
Fully informed	Deliberate	Vigilant
Cautious	Alert	Guarded

WORK

Career	Performance	Vocation
Press, push	Make it happen	A task
Responsibility	Industriousness	Be busy

Top Four Needs

When you have selected your words, narrow your choice down to four. As before, look at the words you've selected and try to arrange them into groups of similar needs. Then look at which words are the most powerful for you.

Once you've selected your four needs, you can check whether each one is right for you by asking: 'If this need were met, would I be more likely to reach my goals with less effort?' If so, then this is probably a fundamental personal need for you.

Connect with your Personal Needs

Once you've identified your four core needs, take each need in turn and write down your answers to the following questions:

☆ Why this need is important to me?

☆ Who am I when I get this need met? (Imagine the need is being totally met. Write down the adjectives that describe who you are when this need is fully met for you.)

☆ How do I feel when this need is not met? (Think about when this need is unmet. Write down the adjectives that describe you then.)

☆ How well is this need being met in my life at the moment? List the ways in which you're fulfilling the need now.

☆ Where is this need not being met in my life at the moment?

☆ What changes am I willing to make so this need is met permanently in my life? Write down three specific changes you will make in the course of the next year to ensure that this need will be permanently met in your life.

Once you've completed this exercise you'll have three action points or changes to make to ensure that each of your core needs is fully met. You must believe that it is possible to satisfy your own personal needs, but it is also important for you to understand that the people who really love you will be willing to meet your needs. I want you to identify two or three people you believe can help you and enlist their support. If you find it useful, you could ask close friends to tell you what they feel your needs to be and see how this compares with your own answers.

Tackle your Relationship Blocks

Having established a clear idea of the relationships you want and addressed the needs that drive you, I'd like you to ask yourself if there are any obstacles blocking your way to creating quality relationships. If you've done a thorough spring clean in Step 3, you'll have already cleared out much of your emotional clutter. Are there any outstanding issues you need to tackle? These can include any unfinished business from past relationships or limiting beliefs you hold that are stopping you from attracting the relationships you want.

Complete and Learn from your Past Relationships

A critical element in developing satisfying relationships is ensuring you break any negative patterns and complete any unfinished business. You might need the support of a trained counsellor to help you here.

People often choose relationships based on a pattern created in their childhood and sometimes select a partner based on the characteristics of their parents' relationship. You might want to look at your parents' relationship to see how it parallels your own experiences and think how it may have influenced your choices. Equally, if there are any issues outstanding between you and a previous partner, friend or associate, you need to resolve these if you want to avoid repeating the same mistakes again in your future relationships. When you feel 'complete' in yourself, you'll be more likely to recognize potentially incompatible partners at the outset and won't be wasting time and energy trying to resolve old relationships in your new ones.

If a person is still on your mind and affects the way you sometimes think, feel or behave, the chances are your relationship with them needs to be completed in some way. If you still feel any sadness, anger, guilt, embarrassment or other strong emotion towards someone, I'd like you to address it. Being aware of unfinished issues in your life is the first step towards doing something about them.

☆ Be honest with yourself. Which of the relationships in your past are still incomplete?

☆ What are the outstanding issues you need to resolve?

☆ What are you resisting or holding on to that you need to let go of?

☆ What are you willing to do to deal with your outstanding issues and resistances? What steps can you take towards resolving them once and for all?

☆ What boundaries can you put in place to minimize the effect of less than ideal relationships on your life?

Address your Limiting Beliefs about Relationships

Your ability to attract the people you want in your life will also depend on how well you've dealt with the beliefs you hold about relationships. I'd like you to take another look inside yourself and check whether you have any limiting beliefs about relationships. If so, revisit Step 3 and work through the suggestions to tackle these once and for all. Don't forget, no emotional state lasts forever – you have the ability within yourself (and perhaps with help from others) to move through any resistance.

Our emotions are proof that we are living, feeling humans. If you feel stuck in a painful situation or with a negative emotion, allow yourself to be present with your pain rather than tiptoe around it. It might not feel comfortable, but when you realize it's perfectly human and OK to be experiencing this, you will allow yourself to learn from it. As you let go and surrender your attachment to your resistances, you'll find it easier to move through them and move on in your life.

☆ What lessons and gifts can you find in the beliefs and resistances you've held about relationships?

Once you've learned the lessons from the relationships in your past, you'll be emotionally free to attract your ideal relationships in the future. Relationships really work when those involved have addressed their own issues, slain their own dragons and have a strong sense of themselves.

☆ *What you leave behind is not what is engraved in stone monuments, but what is woven into the lives of others.* ☆

Pericles

Attract the Relationships You Want in your Life

Now you're fully aware of what you want and are tackling the obstacles in the way of you developing enriching relationships in your life, you're ready to start attracting the right people.

Attraction and communication flow from who you are and how you live your life. People want to be with people whom they can trust, respect, relate to and like. One of the key lessons of attraction is that you attract who and what you are ready for in life. What you give out tends to get reflected back to you by those around you. For example, if you're feeling negative and critical about people, it's highly likely that the people in your life will be negative and critical towards you.

☆ Who are you attracting in your life now? What are the common themes and characteristics in your relationships?

There follows a selection of reminders, hints and tips to improve your natural powers of attraction and communication. Work with the ones that are most appropriate for you.

Be Yourself

When you express your true self, you'll be more likely to attract people on your terms, people who value you for who you truly are. So, dress in clothes that make you feel comfortable, listen to music that moves you and surround yourself with things you love. Be proud of what you do and who you are. The more you do this, the more you'll be giving off vibrations that'll be picked up by the right people for you.

☆ What changes do you need to make to express yourself more fully?

Give Unconditionally

Giving to others without expectation of anything in return is probably the single most important way to attract people and improve your relationships. The giving in itself will heighten your own sense of self-worth and satisfaction.

Think about your own strengths and how you can use those qualities to help others. How can you best support others? What can you give and what do they want? How, by helping others, can you can reach your goals faster and more easily? Tapping in to the power of others can elevate your life. I want you to benefit from the cross-fertilization of ideas, experiences, knowledge and wisdom by first giving of yourself.

☆ **List three ways in which you can give to others.**

Become a Model of What You Seek

Like attracts like. If you want more trust in your life, start by trusting yourself more. If you want more love, love yourself and others more – the chances are that love will be returned to you.

☆ **What characteristics do you appreciate in other people?**

Reading through the qualities you've just written down, score yourself out of 10 for each. Give yourself 10 if you feel you're fully expressing this characteristic in your own life at the moment and only 1 if this is a quality you currently don't possess. It's easier to attract people with specific qualities if you already have them yourself. Think about what characteristics you want to develop in yourself now. Remember, awareness is the starting-point, but action is key! Treat those you meet in the way you want to be treated yourself and this will be reflected back to you.

Acknowledge People and Show You Care

Acknowledging people and showing them you care and want a lot for them is an extremely empowering way to build relationships.

> ☆ Choose three of the most important people in your life and tell them what you love and appreciate about them the most.

I challenge you to acknowledge at least three people daily. Ways of doing this could be sending them a card or 'Thank you' note, spending quality time with them, speaking with them on the telephone, sending them an e-mail, doing something (however small) you know they'll appreciate or arranging an activity to enjoy together.

Ask for What You Want

Don't be afraid to state clearly what you want in a relationship. A common mistake is to expect others to know what you need and want, which is often not the case. When you're able to ask for what you want, you become easier to be with, easier to please and much more attractive. People see you as clear and straightforward. I want you to learn how to ask for what you want in all your relationships. Tell people how they can be ideal for you – it will benefit you *and* them!

Address Problems or Mistakes as Soon as They Arise

Don't overlook problems or bury issues or misunderstandings, but address them immediately. Make amends swiftly and nip problems in the bud before they multiply.

Don't deny, try to justify or blame someone else for a difficult situation, but realize you have the power to change it. Whatever the situation, you can take charge and manoeuvre the relationship onto a higher, more positive plane. Allow yourself to see an upset as an opportunity to learn something, change something or improve matters to everyone's advantage.

Improve the Way You Communicate

Poor communication can destroy relationships or prevent them from developing in the first place! The clearer your channels of communication with those around you, the more attractive you are to them. You can improve your own communication skills, little by little, day by day, by being aware of the importance of communication and then by taking action. Take time to be present in the moment with people and not get distracted. Pay attention to them moment by moment. Listen to them, watch their body language and attend not only to what they say, but also to what they do.

Understand that People's Perceptions Become their Reality

The challenge in communication is that everyone has a different hold on reality based on their own perspectives, information and perceptions. I want you to accept that people are more than just their behaviour. The more you allow yourself to see things from a different perspective and realize that people do the best they can with the resources they have at hand, no matter how you look at a situation there are always two sides.

Be Unconditionally Constructive

Ensuring you say nothing but the very best for people will enhance your relationships. If you have a disagreement with someone, focus on the positive. Don't make the other person wrong, simply provide constructive feedback on how things can be improved.

Understand the Other Person First

Do your best to understand another person first before expressing your own point of view. Don't prejudge them or jump to conclusions. Ask clear questions and listen fully to the answers. The higher the quality of your questions, the easier it is to understand the answers. Listen with great empathy. Treat people with respect and respond to their needs. Put yourself in their shoes and seek to understand where they're coming from. Then, from their perspective, think about the result that would constitute a win for you.

When Faced with a Difficult Situation, Ask Yourself Empowering Questions

☆ Am I willing to do something now to change this situation?

☆ Why have I become upset by this situation?

☆ Could my interpretation of it be a misperception? Do I have all the information necessary to understand the situation?

☆ What else could this mean? (For every negative meaning that you've come up with, can you come up with a positive one too?)

☆ What do I need in order to feel good now? Do I need to change my perception, get more information, understand the other person's point of view, know they care, change the way we're doing something, get a commitment from them? Do I need to apologize or do I need to remember who this person is and how much I really love them?

☆ How can I communicate my needs in a way that empowers my relationship with this person? What is the good thing that has come to light from this?

Mix with People Who Are Good Communicators

If you're serious about improving your communication skills, look for role models and see what you can learn from them. Good communicators tend to have a 'lightness', clarity and well-developed sense of humour. The more you associate with these people, the greater the likelihood that their own characteristics will rub off on you!

☆ Who are the good communicators already in your life?
  What can you learn from them?

☆ What will you do to improve your powers of attraction and
  communication?

Key Insights Gained from Step 9

☆
☆
☆

Quick Wins Gained from Step 9

☆
☆
☆

The Action Steps I Will Now Take

Action	Deadline date
☆	☆
☆	☆
☆	☆

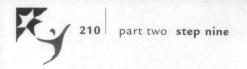

Real Results

Jenny *Head of marketing, single, 30s*

Jenny had an extremely successful career, was well respected and loved what she did, but despite this her life felt empty. She had little time for herself and wanted to find a special partner. She was starting to think there was no one out there for her.

The Value of Coaching
To help Jenny improve her relationships, remove her energy drains, get her needs met and open her up to new possibilities.

> ☆ My Ideal Relationship
> This exercise was a turning point for me as it helped me to see where I was and where I wanted to be in my ideal life. It lifted me out of my day-to-day worries and helped me see things from a different – and clearer – perspective. Traditionally I'd always been attracted to high-flying, successful, hard-working businessmen, who usually seemed to prefer me as a friend rather than anything more intimate or serious. I realized that I wanted a guy who had sex appeal and 'oomph', someone who wasn't so consumed with work that he was weary and tired and life felt boring. I wanted someone with a wide variety of interests, a good communicator who really cared about me and my feelings. The important qualities for me were 'honesty', 'loving', 'giving', 'loyal', 'supportive', 'fun' and 'looking for exciting things to share with people'. I wanted someone who would love me for who I am, who couldn't wait to see me, who respected me, recognized my strengths and weaknesses, would call when he said he'd call and do what he said he'd do – someone who would offer unconditional love.
>
> When Carole asked me to picture my ideal life at the end of the year, I found it quite easy to build an image in my mind of what I wanted. Then I had a major 'aha' – there was no reason why I couldn't have

those things *now*, the only thing that was stopping me was myself and my own negative thoughts. That spurred me on...

☆ My Needs

I realized my key needs were 'to be looked after', 'to be listened to', 'to be important' and 'to be loved'. I knew that unless I started to take steps to get them met before I got involved in a significant relationship, I could put a lot of stress on a potential new partner and maybe even undermine a new relationship. I looked at ways I could get my needs met by my friends and family and in healthy ways at work. As I started to focus on this, I really felt I was taking charge of my life.

Real Results

Jenny addressed her limiting beliefs 'There is no one with any "oomph" out there for me' and 'I may never be able to have children' and adopted a more positive mindset where she acknowledged that 'I will connect with the right guy when the time is right.' She freed herself from only having eyes for a man who wanted her only to be a friend and started to socialize with a wider circle of acquaintances. After addressing her needs, she felt lighter, with renewed energy and vitality for life. Several months ago she met a wonderful new man and is starting to share her life with him.

☆   *A man is not where he lives,*

but where he loves. ☆

Latin Proverb

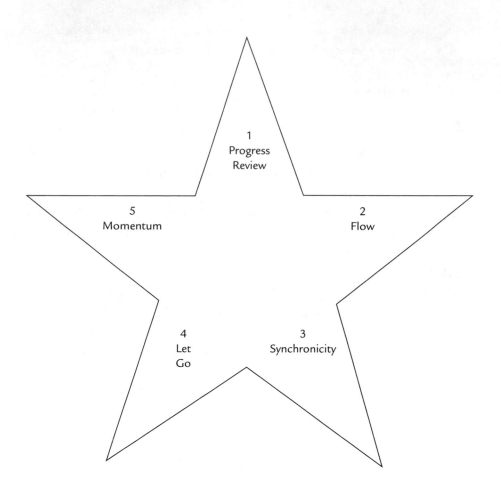

get

into
the flow

☆ *There will come a time when*

you believe everything is finished.

That will be the beginning. ☆

Louis L'Amour

Overview

Scientists tell us we only use a tiny fragment of the total capacity of our brain. Our minds are capable of so many more things than we can currently conceive. In this final step, I want you to suspend all disbelief and open your mind to your own limitless potential.

I know ordinary people can do extraordinary things. Time and time again I see my clients surprise themselves and that's what I want for you! You can achieve anything you believe in, if you really put your mind to it.

If you've now completed Steps 1 to 9 the chances are you're already transforming your life. Keeping your intentions clear, paying regular attention to your vision and goals, and magnifying them, so they become larger in your life, will have a significant impact on bringing them closer to you. Planning your life, breaking things down into small manageable steps and keeping to your plan will ensure you keep moving forward.

Having put all your key elements in place, I want this final step to inspire you to open yourself up to capture that extra magical something in your life that will lift you up to a higher level. There really is no end to what you can achieve!

When you've completed this step:

☆ You'll have reviewed your progress to date and acknowledged how far you've come.

☆ You'll be developing your own rhythm and pace, paying attention to the moment, recognizing opportunities as they arise and getting into the flow of your life.

☆ You'll become more aware of synchronicity and start to take action to make the most of perfectly timed events as they occur.

☆ You'll trust yourself to let go and grow for your greater good.

☆ You'll be celebrating your transformation, maintaining momentum and integrating your new knowledge on an ongoing basis so you are living your life at a higher, more fulfilling level.

Personal Reward for Completing Step 10

☆ Write down here how you will reward yourself when you have completed Step 10:

Quick Transformation Quiz

Answer the questions below by ticking the appropriate box and calculating your score as follows:
2 points = Yes/Agree/Not Applicable, 1 point = Agree sometimes, 0 point = No/Disagree

		YES	SOMETIMES	NO
1	I have a positive outlook on life and make the most of the opportunities that face me.	❏	❏	❏
2	I am happy and fulfilled in my personal and professional life.	❏	❏	❏
3	I am optimistic about myself and the future ahead of me.	❏	❏	❏
4	I am intuitive and trust in my own wisdom.	❏	❏	❏
5	I am open and aware of the things going on around me and fully respond to them.	❏	❏	❏
6	I am appreciative of the things in my life and see the beauty in all that surrounds me.	❏	❏	❏
7	I rarely get tired or become ill and am well connected to my own energy source.	❏	❏	❏
8	I am living my own life on my own terms and feel fully satisfied.	❏	❏	❏
9	I am naturally motivated and inspired and have plenty of energy for the life I want to live.	❏	❏	❏

		YES	SOMETIMES	NO
10	I am open to synchronicity and to the remarkable people that come into my life.	❏	❏	❏
11	I tend to take the path of least resistance and achieve my goals relatively smoothly.	❏	❏	❏
12	I am consistent. People understand me and know where they stand with me.	❏	❏	❏
13	I live a life of excellence and am constantly doing my best in everything I do.	❏	❏	❏
14	I live in the present and simply enjoy myself focusing on things that fulfil me.	❏	❏	❏
15	I am willing to take risks and to trust that what will be will be.	❏	❏	❏
16	I feel totally in the flow of life – it's fun and fulfilling and I'm engaged in creating a wonderful future.	❏	❏	❏
17	If I were to die today, it would be with few regrets.	❏	❏	❏
18	I am willing to experiment and am constantly evolving and growing.	❏	❏	❏

Initial Score ❏ **Score on Completion of Step 10** ❏

Final Score on Completion of Book ❏

☆ *And the day came when the risk it took to remain tight in a bud was more painful than the risk it took to blossom.* ☆

Anaïs Nin

Review your Progress and Acknowledge How Far You've Come

Congratulations on progressing this far! If you've completed the majority of the assignments, the chances are you'll be a different person from the one who started out on the 10-step process!

I'd like you to take the time to review the progress you've made so far and clarify your next steps forward.

☆ What were your most important original goals?

☆ Which ones did you accomplish? (If it's appropriate, give yourself a score out of 10 for each goal – 10 being fully accomplished and 0 being not made the first move yet.)

☆ Of the goals you didn't accomplish, are they still goals? If so, how do you plan to work towards them?

☆ What new goals surfaced as a result of following the 10-step process?

☆ What were the most challenging elements of the process for you?

☆ What three lessons would make the most difference to you if you were to follow them in the next phase of your life?

☆ Since beginning your life transformation process, in what ways have you stretched beyond your comfort zones?

☆ What can you do now that you didn't think was possible before you started to transform your life?

☆ What was the self-belief which had the most negative influence over you and how are you turning it into an empowering belief to move you forward?

What Is and Isn't Working?

By now, your life transformation will be well underway and you'll no doubt be tracking your progress and monitoring your results as you go. As you evolve I want you to pay close attention to what is and isn't working.

Be flexible in your approach. If you're not enjoying something, ask yourself why and make changes accordingly. Your own feelings, energy and vitality levels will serve as clear success indicators and will provide you with clues as to what needs changing. Also, the people around you are likely to reflect what's going on in your life. Be aware of what and whom you're attracting and learn from this.

Get into the Flow

Align with your Natural Energy

Now you've established your progress to date, I want to support you in maintaining your momentum so you get into the flow of your life. Once you tap into the flow, your life moves along enjoyably and seems less of a struggle. You feel 'at one' with yourself and your world, creative and productive and energized by your life and your work. You find yourself in an active state of harmony and integration. Athletes sometimes refer to a 'flow' state as 'being in the zone' – a time when they reach peak performance and when true magic occurs. In the flow, intuition and insights just come to you spontaneously. You find yourself going with whatever comes to you and you are pulled naturally towards your vision and goals.

To get yourself 'in the flow', you simply need to align yourself with the natural energy that is already present in your life. To become 'super-conductive' you need to clean up and streamline your life on an ongoing basis. I want you to keep clearing out and working on yourself so you allow your energy to flow. If you have any outstanding energy drains, address them as soon as you can. Remember, the clearer the space around you, the more room you create to surround yourself with positive energy.

The more you tune into your natural strengths and spend time doing the things you love and the more you top up your life with joy and simple pleasures, the more often you'll find yourself 'in the flow'.

☆ What changes can you make to align yourself more with your natural energy?

Allow Yourself to Become Present in the Moment

Your sense of flow can be developed by allowing yourself to become more present in each moment. Give yourself time to slow down, notice all the details of your day-to-day life and take advantage of the external and internal cues around you. As you pay more attention to your world and adopt an open, receptive state of mind, you'll start to see more and to increase your awareness of flow. This is a time for inspiration and gaining new insights and fresh perspectives on things. When you're caught up in a fast-paced goal-driven life, you can fall into the trap of living in the future and overlooking the magic of the present. But when you pay attention to the moment, you'll probably be pleasantly surprised by the great opportunities that are staring you in the face, simply waiting to be noticed!

Being present in the moment sets you up to take full advantage of unforeseen circumstances. When things happen unexpectedly or you get a different outcome from the one you had originally hoped for, if you're paying attention, you can let the unexpected guide you to a new and perhaps better future. When your life is truly flowing and you allow yourself to be open-minded and let things fall into place naturally, your future can move towards you more quickly than you originally thought possible.

☆ How much of your time and/or energy is being lived (consciously or unconsciously) in or for the future instead of for today?

☆ What changes do you still need to make to ensure you're able to keep yourself focused and centred in the present moment?

Follow the Path of Least Resistance

Once you tap into the flow, you no longer need to push yourself hard to achieve the things you want in your life. Life can become easier and less of a struggle. Think of it like riding a bike. You've spent time and energy planning your route and have ridden up hill and down dale and now's the time to let go, freewheel down the hill and enjoy the ride!

Pace Yourself, Accept the Ebbs and Flows and Don't Give Up!

Whilst enjoying the natural momentum you're creating in your life, don't forget that there will be ebbs and flows. Tune into your inner wisdom and pace yourself in accordance with what feels right for you. The chances are you'll grow and evolve quickly on some occasions and more slowly on others. Give yourself time to absorb and assimilate what you've learned and don't push yourself to move too fast. Remember, you're likely to reach your results through a cycle of ups and downs.

We all go through 'challenging' patches every now and again. Let's face it – we are human! When you're in an inactive place, don't give up – it won't last forever. Sometimes it's during our apparently 'inactive' and 'ugly' phases that we're undergoing our most important learning experiences. Often nothing appears to be happening just before a major growth spurt. Think of a caterpillar becoming a rather ugly, inactive chrysalis before it bursts back into life as a beautiful butterfly. Accept that we must all go through a 'chrysalis' phase every one in a while! Find ways to enjoy your life, accept any lulls you may experience and maintain your focus on what you want.

Pay Attention to Synchronicity in your Life

Is your life full of coincidences? Do you think about someone, only for the phone to ring and for you to find them on the other end of the line? Do you increasingly find yourself in the right place at the right time? Synchronicity, or meaningful coincidence, occurs in your life by means of perfectly timed events that just seem to happen out of the blue. These events may seem insignificant to you at the time, but when you look back later, they're often key turning-points.

Let Synchronicity Work for You

Synchronicity can be extremely helpful in moving your life forward. I want you to allow it to work for you. You can do this by paying close attention and becoming more aware of what's going on around you. As you become more present in the moment, you're more likely to look out for coincidences and start to notice synchronicities in your life. Pay attention to the people you keep bumping into. What do they say to you? Is there a topic that comes up time after time? Do you keep reading articles about the same subject? What keeps happening to you over and over again? Are there any key messages there for you?

Don't overlook the significance of coincidences. Ask yourself what they're showing you. They could propel you forwards more quickly than you might initially realize and are often a good indication that you're on the right path. As you open more to your intuition and inner wisdom, you'll notice synchronicities taking place more often and your life naturally gaining a steady momentum.

☆ What coincidences have occurred in your life over the last few weeks?

☆ What have you done to make the most of these events? Have you missed something significant?

☆ Make a list of the three people who seem to keep showing up most often in your life and what you intend to do to discover why:

4 Take a Leap of Faith and Let Go

Now the path and direction of your life transformation is clear, you've started to take action and things are gaining momentum, you're *in the flow*. A critical element during this part of the change process is having the ability to let go. No matter how clear and well planned your intentions and goals, there comes a point where you have to stand back, surrender and let things take their natural course.

I want you to learn to let go of your attachments to the results you want, take a leap of faith and trust that what will be, will be. Know in your heart that if something is supposed to happen, it will. If it doesn't happen the way you wanted, look for the lesson and accept a different way forward.

Have faith, take your courage in both hands and let go of your need to know, let go of your fears, let go of your limiting beliefs, let go of your attachment to the opinions of others, let go of your expectations of specific results – and trust that what happens will be for your highest good.

Surrender to the flow and you'll come through the transformation process faster. In the long run it will pay you to be bold and courageous. When you look back on your life, you'll regret what you didn't do more than what you did.

Maintain Momentum

Take Daily Action

As your coach, I want you to get into the swing of maintaining your momentum and applying your new knowledge on an ongoing basis.

Moving ahead one small step at a time and taking regular daily actions towards the future you want will create a natural momentum to propel you forwards. Keep your vision, intentions and goals in your daily sight, acknowledge them in written form in your planner and your daily inspiration journal, acknowledge them verbally in your affirmations and integrate them into your everyday life. Expand your knowledge by reading books on related topics, attending courses or workshops and learning more about whatever interests you.

Anchor Yourself with a Symbol of your Transformation

You can maintain the momentum by choosing a symbol that you can see daily to remind you of your transformation. You might like to select an item of jewellery, an ornament or a picture that acts as a constant reminder to you to stay on track.

Take Time Out

Allow yourself time out every once in a while to revisit some of the key insights you've gained from this book. Step back from your busy life and make an appointment with yourself to consciously create the next phase of your life transformation whenever you think the time is right.

Share your Successes

As you make progress, share your successes with your support team and acknowledge the roles they have played in helping you to move forward in your life.

If you'd like to share any feedback, thoughts and results with me, I would love to hear from you. Your stories are a constant source of inspiration, ideas and energy!

Celebrate

I mentioned the importance of celebration at the beginning and I'll mention it again now. Appreciate the wins in your life, both big and small, as this validates you and makes your transformation more meaningful and fulfilling.

Live your life to the full, live it well, have fun and capture the joy in each moment.

Congratulations on completing this phase of your life transformation.

I would like to wish you all the best for a happily integrated and fulfilling life!

Carole Gaskell

☆ P.S. If you'd like to stay connected with thoughts and ideas on transforming your life, you can subscribe to my free e-mail newsletter by visiting my website:

www.lifecoaching-company.co.uk
or e-mailing me at **info@lifecoaching-company.co.uk.**

☆ *There is no security in this life.*

There is only opportunity. ☆

Douglas Macarthur

Key Insights Gained from Step 10

☆
☆
☆

Quick Wins Gained from Step 10

☆
☆
☆

The Action Steps I Will Now Take

Action   Deadline date

☆   ☆
☆   ☆
☆   ☆

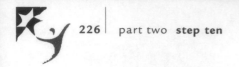

Real Results

Nicky *Recruitment consultant, single, 20s*

Nicky enjoyed her work and family life and had a great circle of friends. She wanted to become more independent, assertive and have greater confidence to climb the career ladder without treading on other people in the process.

The Value of Coaching

To help Nicky to think bigger, live for the moment, be more spontaneous, willing to take risks and go with the ebb and flow of life.

Real Results

"I didn't realize how bored and demotivated I had become at work. Coaching encouraged me to be very honest about how I was feeling, so I took my courage in both hands and addressed the situation. To cut a long story short, I broached my issues with my boss. She was incredibly supportive and I'm now going to head up a key department in the company. I had no idea that anything would change and I didn't ever imagine that it could. Well, it has and I'm very excited about the new responsibilities and challenges that lie ahead. I think I had forgotten how to be ambitious. Yes, I'm also nervous, but I think this is just what I needed. Life is so funny like that. It was almost as though I had to hit an all-time low to come out the other side. I'm back to thinking really positively and things are flowing again now.

Our conversations questioning why things should be 'an effort' are prevalent in my thinking. I feel I now see how to incorporate this in my life and plans.... Things can be effortless if they are the right things for you. Also, paying attention to the moment has helped me to appreciate the small things in life and become more spontaneous in the things I do."

☆ *What the caterpillar calls the end of the world, the master calls a butterfly.* ☆

Richard Bach

further
reading

Step 1: See the Bigger Picture

Daniel G. Amen, *Change your Brain, Change your Life*. Times Books, 2000
Norman Vincent Peale, *The Power of Positive Thinking*. Hutchinson, 1990
Spencer Johnson, *Who Moved my Cheese?* Vermilion, 1999

Step 2: Build the Right Foundations

Jane Alexander, *The Detox Plan*. Gaia Books, 1998
Julia Cameron, *The Artist's Way*. Pan, 1995
Deepak Chopra, *Ageless Body, Timeless Mind*. Rider, 1998
William Dement and Christopher Vaughan, *The Promise of Sleep*. Macmillan, 2000
Denise Lynn, *Feng Shui for the Soul*. Rider, 1999
Leslie Kenton, *10 Steps to a New You*. Ebury Press, 1999
Caroline Myss, *Anatomy of the Spirit*. Crown Publications, OP
Gillian Riley, *How to Stop Smoking and Stay Stopped for Good*. Vermilion, 1997

Step 3: Spring Clean your Life

Pamela Ammondson, *Clarity Quest*. Simon & Schuster, 1999
Brandon Bays, *The Journey*. Thorsons, 1999
Joan Borysenko, *Minding the Body, Mending the Mind*. Bantam Books, 1988
Susan Jeffers, *Feel the Fear and Do It Anyway*. Rider, 1997
Karen Kingston, *Clear your Clutter with Feng Shui*. Piatkus Books, 1998
Phyllis Krystal, *Cutting the Ties That Bind*. Samuel Weisner, 1993

Step 4: Value your True Essence

Gail Blanke, *In My Wildest Dreams*. Simon & Schuster, 1998
Sonia Choquette, *Your Heart's Desire*. Piatkus Books, 1999
Nicholas Lore, *The Pathfinder*. Simon & Schuster, 1998
Oriah Mountain Dreamer, *The Invitation*. Thorsons, 2000

Barbara Sher and Annie Gottlieb, *Wishcraft: How to Get What You Really Want*. Ballantine Books, 1986

Nick Williams, *The Work We Were Born to Do*. Element, 1999

Step 5: Focus on What Really Matters

Laura Berman-Fortgang, *Take Yourself to the Top*. Thorsons, 1999

Cheryl Richardson, *Take Time for your Life*. Bantam Books, 2000

Anthony Robbins, *Awaken the Giant Within*. Scribner and Sons, 1992

Step 6: Clarify your Vision and Goals

Stephen Covey, *7 Habits of Highly Effective People*. Simon & Schuster, 1998

Jinny Ditzler, *Your Best Year Yet*. Thorsons, 1994

Wayne W. Dyer, *Manifest your Destiny*. Thorsons, 1998

Shakti Gawain, *Creative Visualization*. Bantam Books, 1983

Louise Hay, *Power Thought Cards*. Hay House Inc., 1999

Tommy Newberry, *Success is Not an Accident*. Looking Glass Publications, 1999

Step 7: Make Time Work for You

Kenneth Blanchard, *The One Minute Manager*. HarperCollins, 2000

Tony Buzan, *The Mind Map Book*. BBC Books, 2000

Stephen Covey and Roger Merrill, *First Things First*. Simon & Schuster, 1999

Jennifer White, *Work Less, Make More*. John Wiley and Sons, 1999

Step 8: Shape Up your Finances

Richard Carlson, *Don't Worry, Make Money*. Hodder & Stoughton, 1998

Napoleon Hill, *Think and Grow Rich*. Thorsons, 1970

Robert Kiyosaki and Sharon Lechter, *Rich Dad, Poor Dad*. Little, Brown & Co., 2000

Robert Kiyosaki and Sharon Lechter, *The Cash Flow Quadrant*. Time Warner, 2000

Jerrold Mundis, *How to Get Out of Debt, Stay Out of Debt and Live Prosperously*. Bantam Books, 1990

Suze Orman, *9 Steps to Financial Freedom*. Crown Publications, 1999

Step 9: Attract the Relationships You Want

Barbara de Angelis, *Are You the One for Me?* Thorsons, 1998

Richard Bach, *One*. Pan, 1989

Donna Fisher and Sandy Vilas, *Power Networking*. Bard Press, 2000

Criswell Freeman, *The Wisdom of the Heart*. Walnut Grove Press, 1997

Linda Georgian, *How to Attract your Ideal Mate*. Simon & Schuster, 1999

Daniel Goleman, *Emotional Intelligence*. Bloomsbury, 1996

John Gray, *Men are from Mars, Women are from Venus*. Thorsons, 1992

Harville Hendrix, *Getting the Love You Want*. Pocket Books, 1993

Sarah Litvinoff, *The Relate Guide to Better Relationships*. Vermilion, 1998

Ivan Misner, *The World's Best Kept Marketing Secret*. Capstone, 1999

Nita Tucker and Randi Moret, *How Not to Stay Single: 10 Steps to a Great Relationship*. Vermilion, 1997

Step 10: Get into the Flow

Deepak Chopra, *The 7 Spiritual Laws of Success*. Bantam Books, 1996

Wayne Dyer, *Wisdom of the Ages*. Thorsons, 1999

Gill Edwards, *Pure Bliss*. Piatkus Books, 1999

Thomas Leonard, *The Portable Coach*. Simon & Schuster, 1999

Shirley MacLaine, *Out on a Limb*. Bantam Books, OP

John O'Donohue, *Anam Cara*. Bantam Books, 1998

M. Scott Peck, *The Road Less Travelled*. Arrow, 1990

James Redfield, *The Celestine Prophecy*. Bantam Books, 1994

Further Information

If you are interested in becoming a coach, contact:

UK, USA/International

> **CoachU**
> *www.coachu.com* for lifecoaching or *www.coachinc.com*
> for corporate coaching.

UK and Europe

> Carol Golcher
> Tel: 01543 275660
> *Carol@coachinc.com*
> or Sue Wakeman
> Tel: 0121 502 6352
> Sue@coachinc.com

USA, Australia and Asia

> For details about either CoachU or Corporate CoachU,
> call 1 800 48COACH.

International Coach Federation

UK

> PO Box 11853
> London
> SW15 5ZF
>
> e-mail: icf@wonderful-life.com

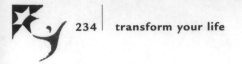

USA

International Coach Federation
1444 1 Street, NW, Suite 700
Washington, DC 20005–6542
Tel: 888 423 3131 or 202 712 9039
Fax: 888 329 2423 or 202 216 9646

e-mail: ICFOffice@coachfederation.org
website: www.CoachFederation.org

About the Author

Carole Gaskell is an international lifecoach, inspiring individuals and organizations to reach their full potential. She helps people to tap into and magnify their own unique essence and integrate their personal and professional lives, so they become more productive, financially secure and personally fulfilled.

Carole was one of the British graduates of the world's leading coach training organization, CoachU, and has extensive business experience in Europe, Australia and the USA.

As Managing Director of The Lifecoaching Company, Carole develops and leads personal and business coaching workshops and seminars and provides contributions to a variety of media organizations.

The Lifecoaching Company offers:

- ☆ seminars, workshops and retreats
- ☆ mini telephone coaching programmes
- ☆ corporate coaching, presentations and away days
- ☆ six-month 'Transform your Life' programmes
- ☆ one-to-one coaching, in person, by telephone and e-mail to leaders, executives and anyone wanting to transform their lives

For Carole's FREE e-mail newsletter, please visit her website: *www.lifecoaching-company.co.uk*

For more general information on coaching and The Lifecoaching Company, e-mail *info@lifecoaching-company.co.uk*

The Lifecoaching Company
PO Box 4596
Henley-on-Thames
RG9 6XU